THE MIDDLE

A Story of Love, Life & Laughter

Nayana Goradia

Published by
Vitasta Publishing Pvt Ltd
2/15, Ansari Road, Daryaganj
New Delhi–110 002

ISBN 978-93-90961-60-3

Edited by Razia Grover
Design by Malini Saigal
Printed at Thomson Press (India) Ltd, New Delhi

To my grandchildren:
Devaki, Selena, Avanti and Ahan

CONTENTS

PREFACE

Nayana Goradia or "Nayana foi" as I grew up knowing her is one of the kindest and gentlest people I know. She is my father's only sister and since I lost him when I was only 10, she formed a large part of the link to my family's generations before me. Her stories were always in incredible detail, remembering everything from the day of the week to the colour of someone's clothes. As I listened for hours mesmerized, I wondered how I would transfer these incredible perspective to my daughter and generations after. I am thrilled that my "foi" has taken on this task and in reading it, see that not only our family heritage but a window into a time that touches on princely states, a Ceylon interlude, bastions of education, the twilight of the Raj in Kolkata in the late sixties and seventies and the evolving political class of Delhi across the years has been opened. The simple, lucid writing style with photographs makes it a nimble read that paints a more detailed picture than it seems to portray.

Aditya Daftary

From left to right: Back row: Madhavi, Aman, Shyam, Brinda, Kevin, Ahan; Middle row: Devaki, Sarla, Sarayu, Darshana, Nayana, Prafull, Gautam; On the floor: Amrita, Anya, Soren, Selena, Aditya

AN INTRODUCTION

The Middle, a short catchy piece, earned notoriety for having seized the centre space on the hallowed editorial page of the Times of India. I began my writing career with this column and though I graduated to other forms, I reverted to the old name believing it invested my book with a sense of enigma it might otherwise have lacked!

This is a collection of my articles—part personal narrative, part imagination, part documentary and part travelogue, laced with humour, satire and tenderness.

The pieces reflect the times they were written in. It was more feudal, more precisely etched, as it were, but also slower and gentler as it was in my grandfather's home in the princely state of Jamnagar. I spent my early childhood in a colonial style mansion with echoing corridors and a profusion of servants, hermetically sealed from the nationalist upsurge outside.

Whisked off to a snobbish school in Sri Lanka in the aftermath of Independence, the under-currents of the Tamil conflict were already around the corner. My not being able to eat with a fork and knife at the school lunch table could bring me tumbling down to the level of a "Demala", a derogatory term for a Tamil, and cast me off from everything in life the school stood for!

In the USA where I went for my Master's degree, while there were students who went on to become Nobel prize winners, there were also those who believed that my weather-beaten gold mojuris were once worn by Emperor Aurangzeb!

After the USA, it was a short, giddy, halcyon stint at Girton College, Cambridge in the UK to register for future research, then it was back home to India.

I came to Calcutta as a bride in the mid-sixties, and began my affair with this glorious, decadent, anachronistic city. Back then, an imperial hangover lingered over the metropolis. Though the Raj had long departed, my husband worked for a commercial house with a British label, and an occasional whiff continued to puff in and out of our lives.

Presiding over the mammoth mercantile houses were the white sahibs living in palladian mansions. The memsahibs were even imposing. But companies had their perks of swish flats in up-market areas, and expense-paid holidays overseas for the favoured. Social credentials were highly prized. It helped to have a father in the Army, the ICS or a zamindar with a title. Sometimes you could inherit an old retainer, left by a departing sahib who would have a veritable Jeeves in the house but also smother your life with outdated etiquette. Then there was membership to an exclusive club with a golf course and portraits of the Queen and her consort and hunting scenes of young men on a pig-sticking spree. At the bar a majestic-looking Abdar measured out chhota pegs, but now a "koi hai" was rarely heard arrowing through the air.

Finally, there was George Nathaniel Curzon, the dazzling Viceroy of India. He may have restored many of our ancient monuments and revived all that was beautiful in our ancient heritage, but he was also the man responsible for the partition of Bengal in 1905 which foreshadowed the larger partition of India and changed the history of our sub-continent! Brilliant, arrogant and handsome, he was asked by Queen Victoria to be her Viceroy. Yet, he returned home a broken man, his viceroyalty abruptly terminated and in shambles. Intrigued, I decided to explore his journey. The odyssey took me to Kedleston Hall in Derbyshire, and other ancestral estates replete with archives and dowager duchesses, who regaled me with stories of the Raj.

My husband was to later teasingly refer to him as the other man in my life. My two daughters put up with slap-dash meals and neglected homework while their mother went in search of Curzon. But finally my book was published in 1992 and remained in print for 20 years. But the word Curzon is still taboo in our house!

JAMNAGAR

A nostalgic recollection of a childhood in a Princely state in Saurashtra where my maternal grandfather as Chief Medical Officer was looked upon as one of the most important functionaries in the state. There was a feudal quality to life. Everybody knew their assigned place in the scheme of things and our days were unquestioning and secure.

Maharaja Jamsaheb comes on a visit.

An Ormolu clock.

Lakhota Fort at the port of Jamnagar.

Map of Kathiawar in the Gazetteer of the Bombay Presidency. (James M. Campbell, 1896)

Coat of Arms of Jamnagar State (formerly Nawanagar).

OF THINGS PAST

The Statesman, 23 July, 1979

When my grandfather passed away at the age of 86 kindly friends said I should not grieve unduly. But in mourning my grandfather, I was also saying a requiem to an era in my own life. It was of a childhood in the Saurashtra town of Jamnagar; in a colonial style mansion with high ceilings and long aimless corridors.

A quarter century has gone by but the remembrance of things past comes swift and vivid to the mind: of high-backed ungainly Victorian chairs lined stiffly against the wall with portraits of pugreed, whiskered, unsmiling ancestors hung above, of Ormolu clocks, stuffed birds in glass cases and a recoco brass bedstead. All this must have been at odd variance with the inmates of the house. But I was not aware of it then. We lived in our smug little oasis hermetically sealed by khus blinds not merely from the heat and dust but also the reality outside.

Over this domain presided my grandfather. He was not one of those round-cheeked, benign, rollicking, story-telling type of ancestors. A highly successful physician and surgeon, he had taken to studying Sanskrit at the age of 45 in order to translate the 3,000 year-old medical treatise, the *Charak Samhita*, into English. To look at he was every inch an intellectual; disdainful gaze from a pair of hooded eyes, on curved nose and flaring nostrils. To meet, he could be intimidating. Impatient of all non-intellectuals, he looked upon them as fools whose chatter annoyed him.

This did not, however, apply to my enchanting, petite grandmother. A beckoning clink of glass bangles from the inner chamber and he would put down his papers to be at her side. My grandmother came from a family of bankers from Rajkot and like all Rajkotwallas may have tended to look upon the Jamnagaris as provincial folk. She had valid reason to do so. In her father's house they had an English lady teacher coming every morning, and the girls were encouraged to play badminton, read poetry and express opinions freely in the presence of male members of the house.

When my grandfather came to see her with a view to matrimony she had been carefully arranged behind a sitar. She was 16 and he ten years older. She had the temerity to raise her eyes to his face and ask about her future home. My grandfather was not a handsome man but the diamond-like brilliance of his intellect must have been apparent even then and she was satisfied with what she saw. He, on his part, was entranced. He is said to have written to her 22 letters between the period of their engagement and marriage.

To begin with, Jamnagar must have been a bleak change for my grandmother. Her in-laws had money but little style. Besides her husband, there was a father-in-law, several unmarried sisters-in-law and a crusty stepmother-in-law in

MORVI

Adjoining Jamnagar and with similar pomp was the Princely state of Morvi from where my father's side of the family, the Daftarys hailed. They worked in the daftar or the offices of the maharaja and hence the name. Some of them rose to lofty positions and today there is a street in Morvi named after them, called the Daftary Sheri.
My paternal grandfather however, was a humble clerk earning Rs 11 a month. He died in 1911 leaving behind five sons and two daughters. My father, the youngest, was only two and it was his elder brothers who reared him.

Maharaja Laghdhir Singh and his son.

My Daftary ancestors.

the house. On her arrival she noticed a clothes line fluttering in the front verandah and in the drawing room, the tables covered with dusty old railway guides. Besides, it was a tacitly understood rule that the ladies of the household would be content to languish in the zenana wing. My grandmother soon made changes. The washing was banished to the backyard, the guides swept into a dustbin and the family made to sit together, albeit ill at ease in the high-backed Victorian chairs every evening.

By the time I came on the scene, everyone had disappeared except my great-grandfather, a plump little man in spotless white dhoti and black frock-coat who sat on municipal committees brooding over household accounts and doting on his only daughter-in-law. She returned his regard. Every evening would find her sitting next to him at the dining table as he had his early supper, her face discreetly covered by a veil. This did not inhibit her, however, from reprimanding him about taking too much ghee with his rice. It was bad for his liver, she would scold. Her father-in-law would agree and wistfully push the offensive item aside.

For all her claims to having an English governess, my grandmother could not have mastered the language too well. The proof being a long-standing joke in the family about the time when Mrs Eleanor Roosevelt came to tea. Apparently my grandmother, in her best pearls and French chiffon had received her in the hall and taken her indoors, Mrs Roosevelt complimented her on her home, spotted an embroidered Kutchi cushion cover and casually inquired its price. My grandmother is said to have majestically answered. "It cost half-past twelve rupees."

My great-grandfather.

My grandmother in dark glasses and stylish chiffon saree with pearls round her neck. To her Jamnagaris were provincial folk.

CEYLON INTERLUDE

At the age of six, I was whisked off to Colombo in what was then known as Ceylon, where my father worked for a multinational firm. My brother Ravindra was born a year earlier in 1944 and my parents felt it was better for the siblings to grow up together. Besides, much pampering by grandparents in Jamnagar could not auger well for the future.

My parents and I.

Pettah market in Colombo in the 1950s.

The seafront and the Galle face road today.

The Ghafoor building in Colombo in the 1940s. It is now a restored heritage structure.

NOT A TIGER POP!

Like many a parent of the time, my father, when it came to his children, was an old-fashioned man. Having left home early, he carried with him outdated notions about the bringing up of children which he had imbibed in his early childhood in Bombay in the 1920s. When he was posted to Ceylon in the early fifties, he carried these values with him.

He had chosen for me one of the more expensive and westernised schools of Colombo, but he also expected me to maintain what he felt was my "Indian" identity which, for him translated itself to outward symbols of wearing bangles on the wrists and a small bindi on the forehead. I hated these outward manifestations believing they would brand me as a Tamil—a people who were beginning to be looked down upon by the Burghers and the Sinhalese with thinly veiled contempt.

But there was no let-up. I took to removing my bangles as soon as my father drove away after dropping me in school, also wiping off the bindi. Somehow my father got an inkling of my defiance. My mother was told to keep a watch on me when I returned home. The bangles would be back in place but the bindi proved a problem. There were no sticker bindis available and I was caught out. I was administered a strict warning. Hot, silent tears coursed down my cheeks. But I could not convey to my father my mortification or my anguish.

Sadly, I could not tell him how I longed to be like the other girls in my class, to be urbane and westernised like them. To go to birthday parties wearing frilly dresses as was the vogue. The paradox was that at my father's urging, my mother had half a dozen silk frocks specially stitched for me at one of the most exclusive boutiques in town! Yet once in a while, my father would suddenly insist that I wear a pavade (an ankle-length skirt worn with a jacket) to a school function. If I protested, I was not allowed to go. I was told we as Indians living in a foreign land should not be embarrassed about following our traditions. Swallowing my inhibitions, I would go to the party dressed in a pavade fearfully conscious of what my friends must be thinking of me. This was not deliberate cruelty. It was my father's way of ensuring I take pride in my Indian identity. He would have been genuinely shocked if somebody suggested otherwise. It was for this reason that on our New Year's Day, my father would deliberately wear a white dhoti. It embarrassed me no end and I hoped our neighbours would not notice and comment.

In today's parlance my father may be dubbed a "Tiger Pop" for what would appear to be his authoritarian discipline. Today's child would not understand that a stern disciplinarian could also be a caring parent putting his cherished child through strict rigour solely for what he believed was his child's betterment.

Though I did think my father was undoubtedly strict and harsh, I never doubted his love for me. If he insisted on implicit obedience and stifled my early rebellion, it was only to groom me for a better future. Why would he systematically snuff out opposition unless it was to teach me to adjust to every situation that I might be placed in later life. I was a girl and, like most families of my parents' generation, believed that my eventual destiny lay in my husband's home. Who knew

My brother Ravindra and I, my father's darlings!

Posing in a lehenga.

where that might be? A girl for her own good had to learn to be pliable, to adjust to any and every situation that she might eventually be placed in if she wanted a happy and secure life. In all aspects my parents were most caring.

When it came to the annual school fete, it was my parents who put themselves out more than any others in the school. They were asked to and voluntarily put up a stall of Indian snacks. My mother would put the culinary skills acquired during her private lessons in Jamnagar to fullest use. She produced plump black gulab jamuns that melted in the mouth, jalebis glistening with golden syrup and saffron strands, samosas of paper thin crust stuffed with a spicy mix of vegetables. The bhel was the most popular item, the little paper bowls getting whisked off the counter in no time at all. For a whole week everything else came to a standstill in our home as my mother got busy with the preparations. First a menu had to be prepared and submitted to the Principal's office for "approval", along with samples of one or two different items. I am told they were devoured with relish but the terse note from the Principal's desk only read "Fine. Will do." With the school stamp underneath.

My mom's friends rallied to help. Vasavada Kaka's wife Urmilla masi and mom would set off on a major marketing spree. Two hundred guests were expected at the fete, though how many would visit our stall, Meena Bazaar, was anybody's guess. My father spent his after-office hours making a placard for the stall. On long evenings he would labouriously cut out paper florets and streamers from crepe paper rolls to hang overhead. Even the trays were decorated with frilly crepe paper edges. All the sale proceeds from Meena Bazaar were passed onto the school. And of course, my parents did not charge for the cost of raw materials!

St Paul's Milagiriya Church, Colombo. "Milagiriya" is the 'Sinhalised' name for the Portuguese word "Milagres" meaning "miracles". The church was built by the Portuguese as a Roman Catholic place of worship and was known as Nossa Senhora dos Milagres (Our Lady of Miracles). Later, it became part of the Anglican Church.

The school motto: "Through the clouds, to the stars!"

The school building behind the church.

A SCHOOL FOR NAYANA

A fashionable Anglican school was selected for me in Colombo. A mile away from the house, St Paul's Milagiriya had a chapel with an imposing clock tower in front. It stood on the main Galle Road which ran like a great artery across the city and then down 60 miles south to the city of Galle.

The T-shaped school building was situated at the back. It housed the classrooms and the auditorium which also had two classrooms in the rear and two more in the overlooking balcony. The Principal was a ferocious-looking Burgher lady called Mrs Janza with a timid daughter whom everybody adored. Every morning pretty Miss Lorriane, who doubled as a secretary to the Principal, belted out martial tunes on the piano as we marched up and down the hall. Half an hour later, having rung the bell, she returned to the Principal's chamber and demurely arranged herself behind her desk. The students returned to the classrooms and lessons began.

Most of our teachers were Burghers, descendants of Portuguese and Dutch settlers. Fair-skined and westernised, they thought themselves to be superior to the Sinhalese and the Tamil, the latter being considered beyond the pale! The Portuguese had arrived in Ceylon in

The pukka Milagiriya girl with her kid brother Ravindra

With my classmates and a teacher at St Paul's Milagiriya School.

Miss Reene looked a bit like this!

1505 followed by the Dutch. Finally the British came with their white man's burden and took charge of the island.

In the pyramid of my father's company, the British Ceylon Corporation, it was the white sahebs who sat on top. My father rose to the position of the Chief Chemical Technologist. Assisting him was his old friend from Pune and Benares University days, Janakrai Vasavada whom he had got to join him in Colombo. I had problems in school. Though I could read and write in English, I could not utter a single sentence in that language. All my education had been confined to private tutors at home in Jamnagar who taught me the fundaments of English grammar but could not speak a word of the language themselves! Initially, I was put into the kindergarten class where I was distinctly older than the other girls.

My teachers were two elderly spinster sisters—Miss Reene and Miss Alwis—both with buck teeth and hair rolled into a long sausage and twisted into a U at the back of the head. I found the lessons surprisingly easy but was tongue-tied and mortified at being different. My problems intensified on the very first day when after two hours of lessons I wanted to go to the bathroom. I did not know how to ask for directions. I was afraid of opening my mouth. What if I made an incorrect statement? Surely those pretty pony-tailed girls would look at each other and make fun? Should I say, "bathroom where"? Or should it be just "toilet"? Or should I simply raise my little finger as they did in Jamnagar. I was in an agony of doubt. Just then Miss Reene came up to me and putting a comforting arm on my shoulder said, "Darling, would you like to go to the bathroom?" I gazed at her in amazement. She must indeed be God's messenger to have divined my need! I could have hugged her then and there because she had been able to peer into my heart and read its secret.

A STORM IN A LUNCHBOX

I GAINED ADEQUATE MASTERY over English and was double-promoted to class II. The other subjects were easier, and I worked hard. The teachers were happy but this quick success caused heartburn among some other girls in my class. Eventually school hours were lengthened from one to three o'clock with an hour's break for lunch at one, and we were told to bring tiffin from home. That weekend I accompanied my parents to the shopping centre at Pettah in the old city. After some deliberation we selected a brand new stainless box with different containers for vegetables and rotis as my lunch box. We rejected the conventional three-tier tiffin box as too old-fashioned. Stainless steel was a novelty and my new box looked smart and natty.

On Monday as lunch time approached, my classmates' ayahs brought forth dainty little wicker hampers. Table mats with crisp white napkins were reverentially laid out on the table. Then came the bone China dinner plates and an impressive array of cutlery. I felt a sinking feeling in the pit of my stomach. My stainless steel wonder paled in comparison. I imagined my neighbours tactfully exchanging glances of muted sympathy.

I picked up my spoon and began valiantly. Just then somebody tittered. One girl leaned over to another on her side and said loudly, and with the cruelty only the young are capable of, "What to do if your parents cannot afford forks and knives? Better to eat with fingers, no? Aaiyo! What is our school coming to? Taking all this Demala people!" The reference was to local Tamils and in her moment of contempt she had stretched it to include Indians.

The natty stainless steel tiffin!

I forgot that the girl was smarting over my repeatedly beating her at class in arithmetic, a subject she had hitherto always topped. Angry tears filled my eyes. I could not see that the others at the table did not share her views. In fact they were shuffling their feet in embarrassment but had not the courage to come to my defence. Stung to the core, I felt myself an outcast, falling from everything I had stood for, everything that made life worthwhile. I rushed out of the door, down the corridor and out of the school gate, brushing aside the gateman's surprised exclamation. I was breaking school rules but blood was drumming in my ears and I did not care. I wanted to get as far as possible from the school and everything it stood for. I ran all the way home. I told my mother she could get rid of the servant boy and the ayah. I would stay at home and do all the housework, but not go back to that school. Then I burst into uncontrollable tears.

Somehow my mother pacified and persuaded me to go back after two days. After that to excel in studies became my singular goal. At the end of the year I stood first in my class with the highest marks. It was standard V. But I did not cease in my efforts to master the English language, the language my tormentors spoke with such fluency and with ease. By class VIII we had all become good friends. I had stood first in both the term and annual exams. My classmates accepted and acknowledged my academic superiority and peace entered my soul.

Our home at 3, Alexandra Terrace.

Brinda goes to visit, but alas! No 3 has been razed to the ground.

ALEXANDRA TERRACE

Our home at No. 3 Alexandra Terrace, Wellawatta, Colombo, situated in a quiet lane in a middle-class neighbourhood, was much smaller than what my father could afford. Within a few years of his joining the BCC, one of Asia's largest multinational companies, my father could have moved into company accommodation, a spacious bungalow set in a garden with a view of the Arabian Sea. But Alexandra Terrace was my parents' first home and they were happy to continue living there. Besides, my father feared that if his growing children would get exposed to too much luxury, it could be corrupting for the soul. So for our sakes, my parents eschewed high living. This was the Gandhian era when ostentation was frowned upon and simple living eulogised. As a daily reminder, a painted portrait of Gandhi found pride of place in our living room. I grew to love our small house and its tiny garden with its guava tree and a passion fruit creeper outside my window. When in season, pink antigone flowers bloomed on the hedge. The floors of the house were of red cement which gleamed when polished with a piece of coconut husk. Chiffon curtains made from my mother's old sarees fluttered from the windows.

The bathroom and the W.C. at the back were in a long rectangular room divided by a tall wall, the window sill cluttered with wedges of used soap and a scrubbing brush. There was no running hot water. It had to be heated with a portable heating rod which would be inserted in a metal bucket and plugged in. The W.C. had a Shanks cistern which had to be pulled with a chain. If you climbed on top you could peer into the bathroom across the wall. A similar arrangement prevailed in the servants' quarter and I remember the roar of anger my ayah let off when she once caught the servant boy peering at her as she bathed from over the partition wall!

As mentioned earlier there were only ten houses on our lane, five on either side, squarely facing each other. At a glance you could see through the main part of the house, from the front to the back verandah, taking in the drawing-cum-dining room wedged in between.

Though we had iron bars on the windows, the main door of the house was only closed at night or on a hot afternoon when everybody was taking a nap. The vegetable vendor came in the afternoon and there was much good natured bargaining. Also the boxwallah carrying his tin trunk on his head. Reverentially he would lay it down and bring forth trays of exotic stuff —exquisite lace, tiny cotton reels in rainbow colours, needles, pins. The beggars came only on Fridays, always neatly dressed with well oiled hair. After one articulate appeal, they would wait silently by the door for the nona to come and give alms. If she failed, the ayah would come by and press a coin in their palms.

By the time my brother was born, the other three Gujarati families had moved away from our neighbourhood. Alexandra Terrace now had an assorted batch of Burghers, Sinhalese and Tamil families. On one side of our house was a Sinhalese family with a pretty adolescent daughter recovering from a broken heart which she nursed by playing on the piano all day. No. 2 Alexandra Terrace was occupied by the Burgher family of Anesley da Silva who worked as an assistant editor in a newspaper office. A big burly man, he lounged around in shorts when he was not at work. His wife Minet, who must have been a beauty in her time, had allowed herself to grow fat, and sat in the porch most of the day, watching the comings and the goings. They had two demure teenage girls, the older one with pink cheeks casting impudent eyes at the boys next door. The da Silvas were the most westernised family in the lane. In the dining room there was a picture of the sacred heart of Jesus. A little lamp was always kept alight underneath. On Sundays the family dressed in their best clothes to go to church, Minet wobbling on her high heels with a straw hat on her head, Anno keeping a watchful eye on his daughters, searching for signs of make-up.

Our Muslim neighbour, an engineer in the railways, was privately referred to as Girigoris because he was built like a gorilla with hairy muscular arms and vast stooping shoulders. On Sunday evenings he would hitch his sarong and squat in the verandah. Thus he would waylay his sons slinking back home after a drink. He would grab at the boy and give him a box on the ear. His roar would bring the neighbours rushing out. Also his wife wailing, “Aioo, how can you do this to your own sons?” The younger children would scatter indoors like frightened deer.

A typical Burgher family in Colombo.

THE AMERICAN ODYESSEY

After graduating in English Honours from the prestigious Elphinstone College in Bombay, I was awarded an international exchange fellowship to pursue my Master's degree (or AM as they called it) at Washington State University in the US. Going abroad was not so common then, so when the news came out, a bandwagon of relatives, neighbours and friends got ready with gift parcels to send to their near and dear ones abroad.

Elphinstone College, Bombay.

A proud graduate.

Washington State University, WA, USA.

ROSSOGULLAS TO NEW YORK

The Statesman, 21 June, 1966

THEY WERE ACTUALLY FOR a neighbour's son who lived in uptown New York. No sooner had the lady next door heard of my coming departure than she took to calling upon us each morning with the determination of an aunt come to stay. With tears in her eyes she would tell us how her Sunil adored home-made sweets, how never a morsel of food passed her lips when she thought of him so far away from home, and how there was not an hour in the day when she was not thinking of him.

On the eve of my flight she asked to me carry a small parcel for her darling boy. It turned out to be an enormous jar filled with rossogullas. Because of her touching solicitude and growing autocracy I dared not question the size of the jar. Besides, it looked harmless enough when wrapped up in an old towel and tucked away at the bottom of the suitcase.

It was only on reaching London that the rossogullas began to invest my journey with a sense of adventure it might otherwise have lacked. During our few days of wandering over Europe I had succumbed to the temptation of buying souvenir knick-knacks which to a tourist truly legalise a journey. They had added to my possessions considerably. I weighed the odds of removing the space consuming towel-cocoon around the rossogullas. There seemed too much of a risk of the sweet sticky syrup oozing through my shoes and lingerie, so I hastily decided against it. The jar had to be carried by hand and that was that.

All seemed well until I encountered a clever little Indian airline officer at the baggage counter who took one look at the rossogullas, grinned and said, "We do feed our passengers, you know!" I laughed but in a clipped kind of way that clearly indicated the joke was in bad taste. But the little incident made me aware of the trouble-making potential of my hand cargo. Stepping aboard the Boeing 707, ancient fears buried since days of drama class at school came leaping to the surface.

The 100 passengers hitherto engrossed in settling down for the flight suddenly sat back and stared the minute they spotted me with my rossogullas. Soon enough whispers were flowing thick and fast. They ranged from sniggered allusions to pickled ping-pong balls to fears that the rossogullas were miniature time-bombs calculated to blow up the plane. The more charitable of the passengers shrugged them off as bewitched duck's eggs to ward off evil spirits.

But they affected most a lady sitting across the aisle. A middle-aged Parisienne, on her way to meet a daughter in Chicago, she sat rigid and silent, prayerfully concentrating on getting to her destination safely. From time to time she cast terrified glances at the rossogullas, obviously fearing that they were jeopardising the safety of the entire aircraft.

When, at Kennedy Airport, I declared nothing but laundry and a jar of home-made sweets the customs official winced as though his credulity had been strained, "Sweets. Eh? What sort of sweets, may I ask?"

"Here!" I said, relieved to hand over charge for a while.

"Yes," he said menacingly, as though his worst fears were confirmed, "I should just about say you had got some sweets!" Producing a pair of unhygienic tongs he opened the bottle, picked out a rossogulla and gingerly laid it on the counter.

"It's edible," I protested.

"Want to try?" he threatened.

"No," I said feeling a little sick.

"Ah!" he exclaimed triumphantly, "I know something's fishy when I sees it or I shouldn't be where I am today."

Three months later I received a parcel labelled "Frozen Foods" from the F.B.I. headquarters in Washington D.C. With the rossogullas was a note containing an apology for the trouble caused and a fervent hope that I was not unduly inconvenienced in my enjoyment of the cute white confections.

AURANGZEB IN ALASKA

The Statesman

It was clear from the start that my Jaipuri sandals were not in rapport with my American co-students at the university. A bright pink in hue, the edges were worked in peacock blue and gold, the sinuous toes curling up to an alarming height. In a moment of weakness I had been persuaded to buy them from a stylish young salesman in Bombay who confidently assured me that Americans would love them.

But, alas! Americans did not seem to wish to have anything to do with them. No sooner had I started wearing my new sandals on the campus than fellow students began avoiding me like the plague. Rumours grew thick and fast. These were clever little jokes about magic, the curled toes being nothing else but snakes petrified by magic.

Alarmed, I wrapped the sandals up and presented them to the matron of our hostel famed locally for her passion for "them antiquities". A middle-aged lady of German origin, she claimed to have inherited her enormous proportions from her father, one of those big bold, trigger-happy cowhands one is always seeing in Westerns. She came back with them, however, the very next morning. Her massive Hanoverian frame spilling over the only inadequate chair in the room, she explained in elaborately polite tones that it was "her mom". For some mysterious reason the sandals reminded the old lady of Red Indian witchcraft. Because of her size and her ancestral despotism I dared not press the matter further.

I then threw them into the garbage can but had to fish them out as the janitor made a fearful fuss. A friendly but cautious soul, he relaxed only at five every evening when he could rush home. But not that evening. Waving the sandals menacingly in my face he said he was convinced they would get him into trouble with the police and deprive him of his job. When I assured him they were but a pair of harmless sandals he winced as though his credulity had been strained.

"Sandals, eh? Then why don't you kinda wear 'em?"

I had no answer. His worst suspicions were confirmed. "Snakes is more likely. Sorta hidden, eh? I knows them snake charmers from your country. Heaven knows when they come like," he said, pointing to the coiled toes.

Eventually, one cheerless winter's night I crept down into the snow-enshrouded, fir-blackened garden and buried the unfortunate sandals. For months they lay forgotten under their snowy siege and I was able to breathe more freely. But not for that long. With the first bud of spring, the gardener, a big fierce man with a moustache like a pair of antlers, accosted me in the shrubbery one day with a tale of a vision that had haunted him all winter. Apparently he seemed to lay great store by Orientals in such matters. Gnashing his dentures he told me it was about a murderous assassin with the devil lurking in his eyes digging up his garden at dead of night. The whole thing reminded him of a movie in which a man murders his wife, chops her up and buries the pieces in the garden. He had overheard the crunch crunch of the murderer in his garden; he knew the exact spot where the relics were buried; and though he didn't dare go near the place himself, he knew that his plain duty was to fetch the police.

To prevent any such calamity, the tattered and torn sandals came back again. They weighed heavily on me, inescapable like the dead albatross. And then one day I got my break. With the beginning of the new semester a student of history moved into the room next door. Mary Anne was writing a paper on the Moghuls in India. Spotting the sandals she gazed at them in a queer, speculative way. "They do look kinda real antique, don't they?" she murmured wistfully.

Quick to recognise the opportunity, I assured her that they were genuine Moghul in fact. As a token of Indo-American solidarity, I even gave them to her when she went off to her hometown in Alaska for the holidays; later I heard that she had presented them to the local museum as sandals worn by Aurangzeb the emperor! It gained the place quite a reputation. The curious flocked from miles around to see the famous shoes; thesis writing students could even be observed standing before the glass case with hats reverently removed.

The Mughal Emperor Aurangzeb Alamgir I (r. 1658–1707).

The year was 1961. The place North Beach, San Francisco, in early autumn. Pandit Ravi Shankar was giving a recital at the nearby Berkeley campus where I was lingering over a university summer session. Panditji did not know San Francisco well then and expressed a desire to a few Indian students to do a round of the literary quarter of North Beach. So off to San Francisco we went!

Ustad Ravi Shankar at Berkeley.

Poetry, music, coffee and long discussions at Cafe Trieste.

The famous City Lights bookstore in San Francisco.

Ustad Ravi Shankar.

Allen Ginsberg at City Lights Bookstore in 1959, photographed by Joe Rosenthal.

WITH PANDIT RAVI SHANKAR IN BEATNIKLAND

The Statesman, July 4, 1971

North Beach was bursting with young Americana dissenting, bizarre, occasionally coloured and frighteningly alive. Instead of wheezy old men coughing into the night, hirsute dilettantes ruminated in street corners, their eyes feverish with excitement. An art exhibition progressed on the pavement, the artist haggling over the price of his masterpiece with fierce energy.

The streets were ragged, as in many other poorer parts of the city, with windblown paper and dead autumn leaves, and the marching phalanx of dull brick houses along the road with smelly babies, unpaid bills and arthritic mothers-in-law. Nevertheless in pubs, barefooted contessas danced in uninhibited abandon to a sensuous Latin beat.

Through the mist-drenched streets we walked, charmed by the gay bohemianism of it all, past an exotic little Hungarian restaurant exploding masses of paprika and to poet Ferlinghetti's City Lights Bookstore where it all first began and which still sells everything from *Kamasutra* and banned pornography to a treatise by the venerable Archbishop of Canterbury.

North Beach claims to be a world that does not believe in Convention, where eccentric behaviour is an accepted norm of life; a world that has amputated itself from the affluent American society. It seemed to be true. Certainly the grey-faced commuters we had earlier encountered caught up in the rush hour of office every morning and back home every evening, were at strange variance with this lotus eating fraternity who lounged in bed all day and awakened to freedom when the world slept.

To our unenlightened eye this freedom meant congregating in cafes, non-conforming over glasses of apple cider and the ardent pursuit of kindred souls of the opposite sex. To work in North Beach is tantamount to being enslaved and to work for money, a highly vulgar Idea.

We drifted into a poetry-reading. Guru-like, the bard was sprawled on a mat, smoking *ganja*. His half-closed eye seemed to brood over the futility of labour. Around him sat a group of intense young disciples as in an Upanishadic ashram with rough woolen mufflers around their unshaven cheeks.

With heavy solemnity he sang about mankind trapped by a success-obsessed society. He enjoined on his listeners to break away before it was too late and to plunge headlong into the Pure Ecstatic Experience. Little of this made much sense to us. But we need not have worried for it was not supposed to. A painted sign on the wall read: "There is method only in madness".

Beats are cheaper by the dozen in North Beach but our poet gave us full value of the experience of meeting one. To look at he was like a tourist guide illustration of the species. He adhered to the convention of non-conformity with great enthusiasm. He was heavily bearded and clad in appropriately smelly, scruffy clothes. His eyes were fanatic and his smile utterly patronising. From time to time he would pause and fix us with his jaundiced Brahmanic eye. We were clearly untouchables, bound as we were by a life of clean, healthy habits, annual visits to the dentist and holidays by the sea.

Considerably subdued we crept out and into

a restaurant next door for coffee, sympathy and rehabilitation of our scattered self-confidence. Here there was little of that sepulchral gloom. A bunch of onions and copper kettles hung from the ceiling over checked tablecloths, with candles in empty Chianti bottles dripping wax.

There were no chairs, only scratchy, splintery benches sawed by a raw hand. With a happy little bump we had descended from the sublime to the earthly plane. Nevertheless, in keeping with the strict protocol of beatnikland revolt against established convention the place was warmed by six charcoal burners as a protest against the crass mechanisation of central heating.

Huddled besides these improvised fires sat poets, writers, critics, sycophants, drop-outs, Marxists, drug addicts, professors, Zen Buddhists, jazz makers, schizophrenics and frauds, who are successful door-to-door salesmen of detergents by day. They talked, ate and drank late into the night. This activity was invested with a kind of feverish urgency as though that time was running out and that the grappling hooks of reality—money to pay the rent and the next meal—would catch up with them. Till then they abandoned themselves to a gay subterranean orgy.

Oblivious to the sound and fury sat a demure old man jotting down strange, cabalistic signs on a scrap of paper. Plump with rounded pink cheeks and dressed in full academic regalia, he was lost in a world of his own. An obliging beatnik from the next table explained that he was formerly a senior professor of mathematics at a well-known American university and about to be nominated for the Nobel Prize when, all of a sudden, Buddha-like, he was appalled by the futility of it all. Promptly he renounced his home and position to live in the wilderness of beatnikland.

The expressive illustration that accompanied the article in The Statesman, 4 July, 1971.

We lingered over our coffee, a little reluctant to return to the chill pragmatism outside, when a young man from a nearby table detached himself from his friends and folding his hands together in a quaint little namaskar said, "I am delighted to meet you, Pandit Ravi Shankar."

Somewhat surprised by this adulation from an unexpected quarter—for the maestro was not so well known in the U.S.A then—Ravi Shankar replied: "Thank you, young friend. Are you a student of music?"

"No," came the short reply.

"Perhaps you are studying at the university in Berkeley, then?"

"No." Again the uncompromising answer.

"What then?" exclaimed Ravi Shankar, considerably perplexed. Initially the inquiry had only been a form of conventional Indian courtesy. The cagey reply had aroused curiosity. "What are you, young man? I mean, what do you do?"

"Do?" cried the beat in great horror. Drawing himself up to his full height he said with scornful patronage,"I am, Sir, a Human Being!"

SIT-DOWNS IN CALIFORNIA

The Statesman

All over the campus, grim, hot-eyed students were walking out of classrooms, squatting in corridors, stamping their feet, shouting slogans, hurling books into fires and generally claiming Rights to Adult Freedom. No sooner had Established Authority in however remote a corner of the earth posed a threat to a human rights, than the whole group of university protesters would joyfully band together to express righteous indignation.

The leader of the revolt was Delgarno, a research student in physics. Rebels were fairly thick on the ground in California but Delgarno gave full value. To look at, he was like a dictionary illustration of the term: bitter reproachful eye, so intense as to compel the most reticent to revolt, a nose like a scimitar with flaring nostrils a thin cynical smile. Besides, he had had Experience. It was rumoured that during his undergraduate years in London he had done a lot of sitting around with Bertrand Russell in Trafalgar Square.

Flocking round the Master was a band of eager disciples whose habit it was to spend their spare time scouring the university, attempting to sway the placid, bourgeois mentality to rebellion.

For a while I managed to remain in a state of intellectual anaemia until one day I was accosted by a lady beatnik in the library. Issuing my book, she leaned across the counter and whispered,"Come to our sit-down on Saturday evening." I muttered a platitude and turned to go, but a blue-veined hand held me. "Do," she breathed in a voice from the tomb, "be sure to come!"

Bitten by curiosity, I obediently plodded over to the given destination. A phalanx of rebels stood upon the steps of the university administration building, breathing nicotine fumes down each other's backs. On a dais higher up was Delgarno calling upon humanity in professional, sculptured gestures to fight for freedom. He scolded the world for its inertia, but only because he was angry it had wasted so many precious years being enslaved by inhibitions.

From time to time murmurs of "Yes, the time has come for us to fight" would be heard among the audience. I was greatly awed by all the superior conversation. A favourite phrase seemed to be "All for the Cause". Then someone brought out guitars and the meeting became a matter of bonfires and carefree sing-songs.

Towards the end of the evening that I realised with a guilty start that I knew nothing about this Cause. I sidled up to a crew-cut undergraduate who from his repeated and vehement assents to the Master's utterances seemed to be in the know of things. Besides, he looked approachable, unlike Delgarno himself. In a sudden spurt of bravery I put the question to him. He was a little taken aback by the frontal attack. And then, "Gee!" he grinned disarmingly, "The Cause? I sure wouldn't know."

HALYCON DAYS

After finishing my MA at Washington State University, I had applied to the University of Cambridge, UK for further studies. Like many students from my Elphinstone College days in Mumbai, to get a chance to study at Cambridge was to achieve a life's ambition. Girton College accepted my application. My idea was to register for post-graduate research, return home, and persuade my parents to let me go back. But that did not happen. I met Prafull, got married and happily settled down to life as a company housewife in Calcutta. When...

Girton College, Cambridge.
A watercolour by the archictect of the college, Alfred Waterhouse.

Floating below the Bridge of Sighs at St Johns College. A must-do for any visitor to this academic Mecca

CAMBRIDGE BLUES

The Statesman, August 29, 1969

A LETTER COMES in the morning mail thickly studded with Her Majesty stamps. It is from a young cousin who has just gone up to Cambridge. I, who was in the midst of deciphering my two-year old's shrill shrieks in Freudian terms, am seized with a sudden, overwhelming nostalgia for those giddy halycon months in Cambridge, for those draughty old corridors in my college, endless and full of brooding Kafkaesque shadows where on freezing February nights I squatted on tepid hot water-pipes desperately striving to revive some warmth.

I remember my first day in college. I had arrived late in the term and no one had warned me of the gay Marxism that locally prevailed, making college gowns—along with bicycles and friends of the opposite sex—common property of all and sundry. Uninitiated parvenu that I was, I bought myself the shiniest of new gowns available. Newly acquired friends tossed glances of tactfully muted sympathy but refrained from saying anything. Full of Twainian innocence I basked in glory spending an awful lot of time flicking off imaginary specks of dust from my shoulders. Alas! A week later the gown was exchanged. In the library. The borrower obligingly left behind his own, a derelict, 17-holed souvenir. But I had been quick to learn the rules of the game and before long was boldly initiating my own exchanges.

❋ ❋ ❋

THERE WAS THE NIGHT when we got caught out after a late and clandestine party. The college doors were closed and our courage was at an ebb when a kindly old tramp came to our rescue. He led us round to a part where the wall had crumbled, heaving us over and to safety. An old tramp did I say? Well, he had looked like one with his ragged tweed jacket and a shabby green muffler round his unshaven cheek. A month later, we were paraded before him for he was an important member of the university senate!

All those cheese and wine parties with trayloads of coppery red apples, polished and luscious, waiting for a Rembrandt to seal them into eternity. Those mellow autumnal evenings when shadows lengthened outside before flickering into dark nothingness while we, stylishly dilettante, talked about the esoteric symbols in Druid philosophy. Or was it the intellectual ferment in Dali's surrealism? Who remembers! No one really knew what it was all about. No one really cared. It was all part of

being young and terribly involved with Art and all that. That was enough for us.

So much in Cambridge has its own particular memories for me. What would I not give just for an afternoon when oncoming spring softly, hesitantly warms the air as we make our way up-river for hot scones oozing butter and home-made raspberry jam; to Granchester, punting past clumps of undergrads untidily sprawled over Trinity "backs" smoking marijuana as they play a leisurely game of snakes and ladders!

* * *

Perhaps no remembrance of things past will be complete for me without sessions with my tutor—an ancient man, genial and well-fed with the flesh folding in deep lines over his furrowed face. As an undergrad half a century ago he had astounded the academic world by an original thesis on the Elizabethan poets, with a promise of many more to come. Reluctant to let a potential genius out of its grasp, his college promptly made him a Fellow for life. He never did a stroke of research again. His driving concern in life became the clipping of a hedge in his private garden and this he did with disturbing regularity, as I read aloud my essay on Joyce's *Ulysses*. His only comment was, "Don't mumble girl. Read up-up". That was all, after all the torture of libraries, dark circles and countless burnt shillings in gas-meters that had gone into making it! I took it back home, my own do-it-yourself memento for the fortnight.

I endured freezing long evenings in dark dank underground caverns called coffee houses only because there was a terrific vogue for that sort of thing at the time. No food was ever ordered, there being too much suspicious speculation about who was going to foot the bill. Hours of starvation invariably lapsed. But I endured them without fainting even once.

All this and much more I survived. It was a part of being young and in Cambridge. It was to us a way of life and we, fashionably bohemian went trooping along.

At Cambridge, I had registered for post-graduate research in English. My special field of study was the avant-garde Irish writer James Joyce who was towering over the literary scene with his controversial novel "Ulysses".

JAMES JOYCE'S DUBLIN

The Times of India, June 16,1968

SUMMER OF 1962 was particularly significant for Joyce lovers as Dublin, the very city which he made famous in *Ulysses* in 1932 and which had outcast him was at last giving him due recognition with an international festival. The hoity-toity from both sides of the Atlantic were descending upon the city for the Joyce pilgrimage. Alas! however, the Dubliners themselves were unaware of this famous son-of-the-soil in their midst and wondered what had hit them!

It was June 16, 1962. In Dublin there were celebrations for a native who had died unwept, unsung by his countrymen. In the very city that had regarded him as an outcast, a museum was now being opened in his name.

No sooner had the news got around than the whole ballyhoo machine of the Arts got to work. Critics and commentators on both sides of the Atlantic committed their snippets to newsprint. And an entire bandwagon of Writers, Reviewers, Artists, Existentialists, Naturalists, post-Realists, Parnassians and Patrons of the Arts began descending upon Dublin like wolves on the fold.

I was at university in England then researching in modern literature and James Joyce. My approach to the subject was considered dangerously bookish and I was told by my tutors to go over to Dublin and stop dead every time a Dubliner opened his mouth in order to listen carefully for Joycean overtones.

I obediently hopped on to the bandwagon. Taking the train up north I discovered the cash register at the ferry station in Liverpool singing a national anthem. The Joyce pilgrimage was certainly *de rigeur* of the season. Our ferry was large, full of diesel fumes and disciples of the Master. There were the Joyce pundits, sallow, elderly men who having once met the Master in Paris now felt they could discuss him with absolute authority; against the railing stood thesis-writing students, gazing over the azure expanse to distant Joyceland; rich middle-aged ladies from Texas dressed like brightly coloured insects cluttered up the bridge tables chattering incessantly about James Joyce. Or was it after all Joyce James? Oh dear, it really was so difficult to remember.

I got to my hotel in Dublin and asked about the Joyce museum and, of course, nobody knew anything about it. "Never heard of it," snorted the stylish receptionist casually brushing me aside as he made way for a grande dame who wished to go to Tipperary. The waiter to whom I next put the question and half-a-crown, leaned confidentially over the table and whispered that this James Joyce must be a myth to lure unwary tourists. For his part, he'd never heard of the man. The chamber maid was convinced, however, he was in America making cowboy movies.

To put an end to the matter I went out into the city. Down the quays where the River Liffey slips and gossips in loose vernacular I crept into a pub frequented by Joyce in the 30s. But the rich tourist ladies on the boat had beaten me to it. One of them kindly pointed out to a harmless-looking little man who sat by himself at the bar, from time to time casting quick, uneasy looks around and checking his wallet, obviously suspecting the company to be out to pinch his Friday pay-packet. The ladies then craned their saggy necks forward, like hens peering out of a coop, to watch the performance.

The man looked disturbed when I settled myself next to him. But it was my question which completely unhinged him. He threw his hands up in the air and raised Cain. He called upon the gods to witness this injustice to him. The rate at which people were asking him about Joyce made him feel there was a nasty plot at hand to get him in trouble. A traitor was Joyce! Aye, that was what he was and had sided with Hitler in the war!

The next three days, I spent alone and palely loitering in Dublin with no one to enlighten me. And then, one morning I spotted a young man on the grounds of Trinity College. An ancient Celtic *savoir vivre* sat upon his brow. Why, he could be a portrait of Joyce himself as a young man. He was chewing straw and reading with close attention *Lady Chatterley's Lover*. Obviously a student of modern literature, I said to myself in excitement. I at once marked him out as a likely saviour and sure enough he had heard of Joyce.

"James Augustine Joyce you would be meaning?" he asked, a little incredulous.

"Yes, yes," I whispered breathlessly, feeling as though I had at last come to the end of my odyssey.

"Aye," he said. "My father knew him in school. They say he was a good tenor. Why, did he make it to the metropolitan opera after all?"

The Raos, old friends of our family, were visiting London and had expressed a desire to meet me. I had dutifully come down to London and dialled their hotel.

THE DISEMBODIED VOICE

The Times of India, May 1,1963

"Good morning, this is Grand Hotel, Kensington speaking" came the voice of the receptionist over the line.

"Good morning," I returned gratefully, "may I speak...?" "Now, then, you'd be calling from The Parisian Beauty Parlour? Madam, would you please send one of your girls over directly. One of our guests, Mademoiselle Du Bay, D-u B-a-y, of suite 117 would like to have her hair set and..."

I finally managed to break in saying, "I'm not calling from any beauty parlour, Parisian or local. But may I speak to Dr or Mrs Rao of room 223?"

"The Raos? But of course, madam," said the inexhaustible voice, "only, why didn't you tell me so from the beginning? Don't worry, I'll put you through to them in no time. Just hold on please, madam."

With admirable self control I said, "Thank you" and was immediately assured, "The pleasure is all ours, madam." I wondered whether to follow this up with another thank you and then decided not to. The receptionist came back on the line with a profuse, "So sorry, madam. It seems the Raos went out a moment ago—just a moment ago! Such a shame, isn't it? Any message? No? Well, do ring back-say-at tea time. They are sure to be back by then."

The Raos were one of those people that my family had known for years and when they learnt that the Raos were passing through London en route to New York, they thought it would be an excellent thing if I came down from Cambridge and met them in London. The Raos wrote to me from Rome to say how eagerly they looked forward to seeing me next week in England. A week later they wrote from Paris to say that as they had got delayed on the way, they had decided to fly straight to New York. Three days later I had a letter from the Raos to say that they were in London for a day or two after all. They mentioned they had put up in room 223 of the Grand Hotel in Kensington. So, within a few hours of receiving this letter, I had come down to London and had rung up the Grand Hotel with such unfortunate consequences.

All afternoon I fed the pigeons in Trafalgar Square and at four I dutifully dialled the number of the hotel once again. I said, "May I speak...?"

"Thanks goodness you rang back, Evelyn. Awful nuisance having the line cut off like this. Anyway, as I was telling you."

I said desperately, "I'm afraid...."

"Never mind, never mind, dear. Do you know....the most horrible thing has happened," continued the disembodied voice with great relish.

"No! What?" I asked unscrupulously.

"The most terrible thing....John and Maysie are getting a divorce!.. there's this man that Maysie met in her office, if you please... he's old enough to be her father, they say... but, he has...."

The last time I tried to get through to the Raos, I was fortunate enough to get the right number. But before I could say anything more than "May I speak to...?" the receptionist told me with brisk peremptoriness that they were getting quite fed up with the whole lot of us at The Parisian. The hairdresser hadn't yet turned up and Mademoiselle was absolutely furious and....

I explained with whatever patience that was left that I was not calling from *The Parisian*, and, could I not speak to Dr or Mrs Rao of room 223. The receptionist said they never had a Dr and Mrs Rao in their hotel. I said they were there this morning. So, she checked up for me and said they were out.

A week later I heard from the Raos from New York. Apparently they had come up to Cambridge at the same time I had gone down to London to see them. They wondered where on earth I had been all day.

A GREEK ENCOUNTER

The Statesman, August 4, 1981

I WAS A SLIP of a student in England then and had written home to say I was planning an Easter vacation in Greece. Instantly alarmed and fully convinced that the place was oozing with handsome young Apollos full of bad intentions, my grandmother had insisted I stay with some old acquaintances settled there. They were an orthodox Hindu business family controlled by a widowed and childless uncle who had imported several young nephews from Bombay to help him in his vast commercial enterprise. What was particularly commendable, according to my grandmother, was that the family had remained untouched by corrupting Western ways.

The Parthenon

Nevertheless, this background had not quite prepared me for a home-away-from-home in Athens that was forever India. A young daughter-in-law, with her head demurely covered, had greeted me at the door with folded hands. Indoors, on the walls were hung large gilt-framed portraits of unsmiling, pugri-clad ancestors, all of whom were garlanded with swags of sandlewood shavings and gold ribbon. On the massive glass-topped dining table at the back of the room was a marching file of stainless steel thalis. To complete the illusion was the Brahmin cook in a grubby dhoti, squatting on his haunches on the kitchen door-way, flicking at imaginary flies. I had to keep glancing out of the window at the silhouette of the Parthenon to remind me that I was actually in Athens and not in Bombay.

But it seemed that the family had made some concession to the locale. Later in the day, I noticed a somewhat heavily-painted Greek woman in a clinging lettuce-green dress rearranging the knick-knacks on the mantelpiece. Well past the first flush of youth, she had black eyes that popped like olives. She gave me a glance of prickling curiosity and asked the daughter-in-law some questions in rapid Greek. Apparently satisfied she gave me a dazzling smile and went back to her work. I was about to congratulate my hostess on her amiable housekeeper, when we were interrupted by the loud arrival of the menfolk of the house for lunch.

There were the nephews, large strapping creatures with loud voices, smelling of violet-scented hair lotion. The uncle was more mild-mannered; a balding soul with a comfortable potbelly and hair growing from his ears, a man who looked as though he would be clearly more at ease in a dhoti and kurta than his expensive American suit. The cook, kindled into sudden activity by their arrival, darted from kitchen to dining-room, like Charlie Chaplin in his silent movies, slapping hot puris onto our thalis. The Greek lady had in the meantime settled down to a solitary meal in the back verandah. I took it to be a clear case of the East being East and never the twain should meet. But I was wrong. Suddenly the Greek lady gave a screech of the ear-splitting variety. The nephews stopped eating and stared at her. Apparently the uncle, having completed a satisfactory meal had emitted an unusually loud burp.

The Greek lady pushed her chair with schooled deliberation, cast a glinting eye at each member of the party at the table, walked up to the uncle seized him by the scruff of his neck and shook him thoroughly. Completely aghast, I asked, "What is happening?"

Helpfully, the nephew translated the conversation in whispered tones: "She is saying 'Why you belch? How many times I tell you gentlemen not belch?'

"Uncle is saying, 'Sorry! Sorry! Please forgive!'"

"She is saying, 'You promise? Never again'."

"Uncle is saying 'I promise. Never again'."

At last she gave him a melting smile and planted a loud kiss on his bald pate.

Seeing my look of utter stupefaction, the nephew added. "Did you not know? She is our new aunt!" Apparently, the uncle had met her at a dance-hall and brought her home as his bride.

A KNIGHT-ERRANT FOR ME

The Statesman, May 1, 1976

My first brush with Equal Rights was during my student days in Cambridge when the university's female population had finally managed to storm the last of the male bastions—the debating union.

Victory was sweet but had off-putting side-effects: these we discovered a week later while punting down the River Cam. Equal Rights were rather rudely thrust upon us by our hitherto chivalrous male escorts who had traditionally and without complaint punted us while we languished picturesquely among the cushions. Midstream, they handed us the oars with, "Your turn to row now, ladies!" Needless to say, the experience was not very pleasant.

Therefore, when as a dewy-eyed bride I came to set up my home, I was determined to be the un-emancipated woman of our little abode, happy to do obeisance to my husband as the king of the castle. He would be the male chauvinist bread-winner and I the captive wife content to dissipate his income, each taking the other's lot as predestined and irrevocable. Let him tackle all the world-shaking problems—how should Dr Kissinger settle with the Russians, the future of the pound sterling, and air pollution. I would look after more mundane affairs—manipulation of the domestic budget, where to spend our holidays and which relatives to invite to dinner. This arrangement was made almost 12 years ago and I have had no reason to regret it.

Alas! The growing tyranny of the self-appointed freedom fighters of Women's Lib is catching up with my placid world. I am now assailed by doubts as to whether or not to love my husband, children, home and cooking. Should I insist that my husband take his share of domestic chores and, in the process, wreck the kitchen? Or, should I farm out my children to antiseptic crèches while I take up a career? Or should I switch roles, as advised by my Revolutionary sisters, and have a husband who will keep house while I go out to bring in the monthly pay-packet? This, I am afraid, is not quite my idea of liberation.

Perhaps it is the best-of-both-the-worlds variety of freedom that we are after. In that case we might do well to borrow a leaf from our grandmothers' books—those exquisitely pampered, frail-looking little ladies who held such total and effortless sway over their homes, husbands and children. How disdainful they would be of the militant Boadicea-like approach of the Woman Libber who believes in seizing her man by the scruff of his neck, brandishing a rolling pin in his face and send him scuttling to the scullery.

Our grandmothers were supreme practitioners of strategy—the indirect approach. They ardently applied themselves to the art of acquiring a helpless, tender, fragile-so-handle-me-with-care look. They hung onto their husbands' utterances as though they were the Gospel Truth but, at the same time, developed a knack for swooning convincingly whenever a verdict went against their whim. Their Machiavellian methods paid handsome dividends. Their men-folk, those fierce-looking, mustachioed men, forced into the position of being knight-errants, gallantly played their part. It has not quite worked that way with me.

Punting down the river is not a picnic!

Etiquette, or how to manage the best of both worlds?

EXILES

The Times of India, September 22, 1963

We are the strangest of creatures. We go abroad only to spend our spare time tracking down fellow Indians and telling them how much we miss home.

Before we leave our native shore, we tell everybody how we are simply dying to be off and once we are there, we cannot wait to come back to the near and dear ones we have left behind.

Our temporary Home away from Home, whether it be an apartment or a room in a hostel, we swiftly turn into a cosy little retreat which is forever India. We try to obliterate the Westernness of our rooms by adding the Oriental touch, an effect acquired we feel through a scattering of all those knick-knacks which only foreign tourists buy in India. Pink plaster-of-Paris models of Hindu gods adorn our mantelpiece, a 'bleeding' bedspread from Madras covers the divan, powerfully scented incense sticks smoke merrily, mirror-work embroidery pieces are spread over tables and walls, an exquisitely carved coffee table which viciously snaps shut whilst in use is strategically placed in the middle of the room, tall birds of inconceivable species made from deer horn stand on a shelf staring moodily into space.

On our bookshelves are the *Bhagwad Gita, Hindu Way of Life*, *An Introduction to Yoga*, *Quick Guide to Indian Art and Culture*, *Palmistry in Ten Easy Lessons* jostling with *Solid State Physics*, *The Gomberg Reaction*, *Theory of Numbers*, *Organic Chemistry of Transition Metals* and *Spectroscopy*.

We talk to local inhabitants only during university forums and at seminars and at Christmas, which is when those committees dealing with promotion of international goodwill become suddenly active and pack us off to the homes of natives, so that we can capture the true essence of the spirit of universal brotherhood. Of course, there are other occasions when we come in contact with them, such as when we are called upon to speak on some aspect of Indian life to a local culture-conscious group. Then we tell them how hollow and superficial their culture is whilst ours is so very traditional and spiritual.

Otherwise, after lectures and tutorials we go off to discover new spices for curries. We explore sinister Chinese and Greek sections of the city in search of green coriander and fresh ginger. The more enterprising of us write cross-country to likely stores which may stock masur and urhad dal. In the evenings we huddle in our rooms or in the rooms of fellow Indians, complain of the cold and the lack of servants, and concoct new methods of making curry. In the outside world President Kennedy may have given an ultimatum to Mr Khrushchev and the Chinese may be penetraring into Assam, but all this fades into insignificance once we start talking about who made halwa with what for the Diwali dinner held under the auspices of the Indian Students Association.

Gift Parcels

To supplement our supplies, every month, we arrange to receive from home parcels containing curry powder, home-made sweets, sweaters knitted by spinster aunts, and a further stock

of shoe-shaped ashtrays and handloom ties to be given away as presents. Before we leave the host country we do a spot of sight-seeing. We load ourselves with cameras and light meters in order to take shots of much photographed places, so that on our return home, we can weary our friends and relatives at length by a display of these pictures.

Once we are eventually back in the midst of the curry and the near and dear ones we had sorely missed, we only wish we could return to dear old New York or Chicago or whatever it was we had left behind. We suffer from 'Foreign-Returned Blues', our eyes are shadowed with the pain of nostalgia, and we feel oh-so-very-unsettled. We find the heat frightfully excruciating and wonder how on earth anyone can ever get anything done here. If we are ever asked about the weather out there, we reminisce with a far-away look and say, "The cold? Ah yes. Certainly it was cold, but it was so very invigorating."

Our accents, like our food habits, undergo a startling change the moment we touch the native shore. Now we can speak only English or American and have the greatest difficulty in articulating a whole sentence in the mother tongue. When loving friends and relatives serve us with home-made sweets and savouries, we sadly but firmly say that these things have now got out of our system. If they would not be offended, we would much rather have a sandwich and a glass of milk.

Having spent a year or two in America, we feel we are authorities on the Western Point of View and the Western Way of Life. The Cuban Affair? There is scarcely an aspect of it we are not competent to discuss in the fullest detail. Jazz? We simply love it. We could spend days and nights listening to it. Dave Brubeck? Louis Armstrong? No, we have not heard of them. Are they any good? Modern Art? Why, we think it is fantastic. We wouldn't miss an exhibition of modern paintings for the world. No, we have not seen the Guggenheim Museum nor the Metropolitan Museum of Modern Art in New York.

When people ask us how it feels to be back, we reply with pale, heroic smiles that if they want an honest answer, we'd rather be back amidst our American friends and our American Way of Living which we have grown so accustomed to. But, it is our duty to stay back and look after our old parents and help our country in this hour of need. No doubt there are others (we would just hate to mention them), who would think nothing of running back to the comfortable security of life in America, but we cannot do that. It is our duty to stay here and nothing, nothing whatsoever, can sway us from our duty.

After talking in this vein for awhile, we leave the task of national upliftment to more dedicated souls and quietly slink back to America where once again we spend our spare time devising more ingenious methods of making curry and addressing local groups on India's Ancient and Noble Heritage.

A SUITABLE BOY

I felt I was at odd stage in my life. I had returned home after two years abroad, was nearing 25 and had not settled in a career commensurate with my qualifications nor with any decent prospects of marriage looming on the horizon.

In January I joined the *The Times of India* as a trainee journalist, signing a contract for five years. My colleagues were straight out from college and none of them had any foreign qualifications. Friend Rahul Singh from Cambridge had been taken as an Assistant Editor while I had to reconcile myself to being an ordinary trainee journalist. But then his father was Khushwant Singh and I had no such connections. But dabbling in newsprint was exciting. I soon made friends with my colleagues, some of whom have remained friends to this day. The terms were, the Company trained you to become a journalist, for the first year after which you were obliged to work for the Company for the next four years. You were liable to return the Rs 3,600 that you earned as a stipend in the first year if you renege on your contract!

My father had happily agreed to the terms believing such an agreement would keep me both usefully and pleasantly occupied until and when a suitable match turned up and we were free to decide on the next course of action. It was implicitly presumed that I would be living in Bombay after marriage and that my spouse and his family would have no objection to letting me continue with my profession if I so desired.

Marriage of course was the ultimate goal though there was no undue pressure from my parents. I too generally accepted the situation and no longer raised violent objection to my parents going off to meet prospective grooms and their families. I only drew a line at my being dragged into the proceedings. My parents respected this and tactfully arranged with my cousin and her very considerate husband to take me and the suitor out to a restaurant for a meal, when the situation arose. This suited me better and I felt I was more on neutral ground, not on exhibition parade as it were.

On one such occasion I was introduced to Munish (name changed). On paper his qualifications were impeccable. Only son of a distinguished judge, his sister was married into an equally eminent family of bankers with a baronet for a father-in-law. Munish had gone to a school in England and graduated with an engineering degree from Bristol. Of slight build, Munish had a pink complexion and spoke haltingly like an Englishman. My brother-in-law, aware of my mild weakness for everything British, thought we had made a catch.

After one of our routine evenings out, Munish escorted me up the stairs to my grandparents' flat where we were then living. My grandmother was up. She greeted Munish warmly and to my embarrassment started tracing the family connections. But later she told my mother that Munish looked like a boy who had lost his mother! It was true Munish had no mother but what my grandmother meant was that he had a forlorn, lost boy look which did not augur well in a prospective groom.

There were others on the horizon. One was studying for his final MBBS and lived on Marine Drive. His father had known mine and his family seemed keen on the match. So much so that they took to inviting me to their home on the slightest pretext. Whether it was to endear themselves to me or to thus surreptitiously introduce me to visiting relations we never did find out. The family seemed nice enough but I was not interested. There was another doctor who had an FRCS degree from London and Edinburgh. But he lived in suburban Matunga, a part of the city which alone in my newly found snobbery, I felt was sufficient reason to reject him!

In the meantime I was also doing my own private research. I was dazzled by the smart young men who had recently come down from Oxbridge with their superior sort of manner and a general air of nonchalance. They lived in elegantly furnished flats in the fashionable southern part of Bombay where mothers in printed chiffons poured tea from a silver service while a uniformed bearer hovered in the background. To me this seemed the last word in sophistication. It did not matter that these were company flats which had to be vacated when fathers retired from their multinational jobs and the family moved to suburban Pune or Chandigarh where the rupee ran longer.

My cousins had married very well, Sarayu to the eldest son and heir of Lalchand Hirachand, Chairman of the Walchand Group of industries, one of the top industrial houses in the country.

Then there was Sarala, the only daughter of my elder uncle Gauri Shankar. Five years older than me, she was sent to Bombay's fashionable Cathedral School. She learnt to speak English with an accent, wear shorts at home and turn up her nose at the hoi polloi. At 21, Sarala was married to Harsukh Kothari (known as Natubhai to the family), a University of Michigan engineer. His father Narbheram had made millions in trade in Rangoon before the Second World War. Back in his hometown in Rajkot, Narbheram built a grand mansion stylishly naming it Nawalkunj after his third wife who was Natubhai's mother. Nawalkunj proclaimed the family's prosperity far beyond the shores of Rajkot.

Sarayu's sister Rashmi also married well. Petite and pert, she had charming dimples that lit up her face. A stickler for fashion, she even matched her hankies with her sarees. Her husband Sanat was a neurosurgeon and one of a family of seven sons known for their brilliance. Their father, Justice Bhagwati rose to be a judge in the Supreme

Court though he failed in his ultimate ambition to be the Chief Justice of India

The future did not seem to look so rosy where I was concerned. A snobbish though well-meaning elder statesman of the family would talk to my mother about the "A1 boys" in the marriage market. His own sons ranked very high on the list, having gone on to top universities like Cambridge and MIT after having schooled in England, all which ensured highly placed jobs with top companies. Maganbhai (name changed) happily chatted about them, secure in the knowledge that ties of kinship precluded my parents pushing my candidature. In those days a "foreign-returned" label was almost a must as it were, and the more well-known the educational institution the more highly priced the groom. An influential banker, Maganbhai was in regular touch with the top industrialists in the city and he seemed to have a dossier on all the eligible young men in town. To what purpose I never figured out. Because he had no daughters himself except perhaps it gave him a sense of power to have anxious mothers of daughters turning to him for guidance, consolation and support.

But it was clear from Maganbhai's talks that these eligibles were not for me. I neither had the connections nor the colour of skin to qualify, though fortunately this awareness had not quite dawned on me at that stage.

Time was also running fast. I was three months short of my 25th birthday. My mother. who had stayed with me in Bombay for the last six months partly to end her quest for a suitable boy, camouflaged this wish by talk of filial duty towards her aged parents. Now the time had come for her to return home to Colombo with my father.

Just then we had a visit from Vinod Parekh, a distant relative who had done very well in Calcutta's commercial circles. Risen from a humble beginning, Vinod had become head of one of the oldest and most reputable British tea broking firms in Calcutta. Besides, he had the good fortune to marry lovely Lolly, the younger daughter of Shri C.K. Daphtary, the former Attorney General of India.

My parents had met Vinod and Lolly when they were in Sri Lanka on their honeymoon. I was then 13 years old. The Parekhs had lived in the stylish Mt. Lavinia Hotel, but repulsed by the cooking medium of unrefined coconut oil, they had started coming over to our house for meals—a not unusual phenomenon. Most Gujarati visitors to Sri Lanka encountered the same problem and I remember scores of hungry visitors gratefully partaking of my parents' hospitality. The Parekhs returned to Calcutta and thereafter we had no contact for many years until on my return from abroad when we bumped into Vinod at a wedding in Bombay.

Vinod Parekh and his wife — the match-makers.

THE BOXWALLAH

Prafull (extreme right) with the Boxwallahs

My parents were in Bombay in search of a suitable boy for me. Just then we had a chance visit from Vinod Parekh, a distant relative who had done very well in Calcutta's commercial circles and risen to head J. Thomas + Co the oldest and the larget tea broking firm in the world.

Back in Calcutta, Vinod must have thought over this problem and zeroed in on a young colleague called Prafull Goradia whom he had personally recruited for his firm some years back. Prafull was the only child of Dwarkadas and Manjula Goradia, a highly respected couple of Calcutta. The Goradias hailed from Jaffrabad in Kathiawad and Prafull's grandfather had been Divan of Morvi where incidentally, my grandfather had worked as a clerk.

Now over to Prafull for this part of the story. (Excerpt from his book 'Fly Me to the Moon', Bloomsbury, 2017)

I FIRST MET MY WIFE Nayana, when she was not yet twenty-five and I but two years older. I was having tea at the Calcutta Club with Vinod Parekh and some colleagues when he suddenly said to me, "Prafull, I believe you are going to Bombay for your vacation." When I nodded, he said, "Do look up the Daftarys while you are there. They have a nice daughter."

I spent four weeks in Bombay, and three days prior to my return dutifully telephoned the Daftarys and went to call on them. I walked in at the appointed hour and felt all eyes in the room turn in my direction and everybody becoming palpably conscious of my presence. There were Nayana's parents on a visit from Colombo where her father worked for a multinational company.

There was Nayana herself, having just returned from her place of work, where she was doing a trainee journalist's job at *The Times of India*, and her grandmother. I later learnt the family on both sides comprised of highly placed professionals, and were well thought of in Bombay circles. Nayana herself had only one brother, five years younger than her.

After the initial surprise—Vinod had not warned them—the Daftarys were exceedingly amiable. The grandmother thawed when she heard that my grandfather had been the Divan of Morvi, the state where Mr. Daftary's father had once served as an accounts clerk. I saw her exchange a meaningful look with her daughter.

When it also transpired that my mother and Nayana's mother Savitriben had been at Wilson College, her father declared, "You must come over for tea tomorrow. I am sure the two ladies would like to meet!"

I could see that Nayana was not enthused. She later told me she had taken me to be one of those typical boxwallahs whose name would be twisted to its closest English equivalent, one who spent weekends at the club playing golf. I told Nayana's father I would convey the invitation to my mother, but as I had no plans for matrimony at the stage, I did feel it was not fair to raise expectations. I had done my duty to Vinod Parekh and that was it. The parents telephoned several times during the day but my mother had been coached by me to say that I was out playing golf. Two days later, we returned to Calcutta, without meeting the Daftarys a second time. When my mother asked me what I thought of Nayana, I truthfully replied I hadn't taken much notice as I was only performing a duty. The answer must have pleased my mother because though she was keen to get me married, subconsciously she was not ready to forgo her premier position in my life.

Two months later, the company sent me to Cochin on a brief posting. I took a longer route via Bombay. Subliminally, I wanted to meet Nayana again so I had written a note asking if she would have dinner with me. I found myself a little anxious about the response, because I had not been exactly forthcoming with the Daftarys the first time round. Surprisingly, Nayana agreed and when I went to pick her up, her parents told me that their niece Sarala and her husband Natubhai had invited me to dinner the next evening at the Ambassador Hotel. It later transpired that the dinner had been arranged as a precaution in case the plans for the first evening misfired. They need not have worried. I was in a mood to take things forward.

I took Nayana out to a Chinese restaurant for dinner. She told me she had also studied at Elphinstone College although three years after me. Subsequently, she had gone to the USA to study literature and journalism, spending some time in Cambridge, England, before returning home. We had a lively evening and I felt something melt inside me. The charms of bachelorhood seemed to fade in the background and I felt myself drowning in her beautiful eyes.

I asked if we could meet again the next morning for coffee, to which she agreed. That was when I proposed marriage. She was stunned. There had been none of the customary preliminaries: the parents' playing go-between, the family interventions, the interrogations, the matching of horoscopes, all the other fact-finding missions. Mine had been an uncompromising commitment. What about your parents, she had asked. I said

The newly-weds. Does Prafull look the hen-pecked husband?

was brushing aside the preliminaries.

Not allowing himself to get disconcerted, Natubhai now turned to his own candidate, propping her up to meet a barrage of questions that I, as the groom, may put to her.

To break the ice, he said, "I believe you were in college together." I said that we were but had not met then.

Natubhai quipped conspiratorially, "Ha! Ha! Then we may not have had to meet like this today!" The assumption being that had I met Nayana then, we may have tied the knot long ago!

Nayana remained totally silent through the exchange. This was beginning to bother her people. Natubhai gave her a neat little kick under the table when he thought I was not looking. He said, "Talk Nayana, talk; what is wrong with you today?" A pity to let an eligible groom slip out of grasp, simply because of a lack of responsiveness from the girl.

Taking the cue, Salem also nudged Nayana and whispered, "Where is your tongue today? Otherwise you talk nineteen to a dozen." They had obviously known Nayana through her growing years.

Salem's charming wife Gala, keeping an eye on me, whispered to Nayana, "He's very nice. Don't let him get away. Otherwise you will land yourself with some typical Gujjubhai..." But Nayana continued to remain tongue-tied. At one stage, she had looked beseechingly at me. But by now I was enjoying myself. The scenario was evolving in my favour. The family was on my side.

A year later, we were married on a tiny plateau of land overlooking the Arabian Sea.

they were in the know and had said they would be happy with my choice. What about the relations in Bombay—the grandmother, uncles and aunts? I said it would not be fair to state her decision to them until her mind was made up. I myself had no doubts. The decision now had to be hers. After that, she had gone silent.

That evening I was on my best behaviour. Donning my best suit and shirt, I punctually turned up at the Ambassador Hotel. Apart from Nayana, there were two other couples present: one I guessed to be Nayana's brother-in-law and cousin, and the other I learnt were Gala and Salem Cohen, old family friends specially invited to smoothen the course of making the match.

"Goradia is my name," I said in my smoothest anglicized accent, stretching my arm out to Natubhai.

He looked a little nonplussed at my jauntiness. He was used to being the master-of-ceremonies on such occasions, going out of his way to put the prospective groom at ease. But here the groom

CALCUTTA: AN ARTIST'S IMPRESSION

Pen and ink sketches by Desmond Doig

The Strand near Fort William. Job Charnock landed further downstream, and the first fort is where the G.P.O. is now. The indomitable Rani Rashmoni once had an iron chain slung along the river near this spot to obstruct the passage of the English ships.

The old and the new: A 19th century bird cage juxtaposed against a new skyscraper!

CALCUTTA OF THE MID-SIXTIES

Courtesy: 'Fly me to the Moon' by Prafull Goradia

IN THE MID-SIXTIES, an imperial hangover continued to hover over Calcutta, and particularly over the world of company executives. It seemed as though the British had converted Calcutta into their home-away-from-home-which-was-forever England. As in London, Calcutta had its open parks, the Maidan at its heart; the Hooghly river breeze brought along with the salt air, as did the Thames, the aroma of spice and tea. One could see huge neo-classical mansions standing amid carefully cultivated gardens facing wide boulevards; public buildings had been created to appear awesome, the grandiloquent style heightened by Palladian facades and columned doorways. The old families lived in imposing mansions in the north of the city. Some of the buildings there were, however, now splitting apart under the hammer blows of taxation and neglect.

But old colonial institutions like the clubs, which had started taking in Indian members, were acquiring a growing momentum. These clubs were now bustling with Calcutta's young, bright, inexhaustible and modern men and women. Everywhere around one could sense the colonial presence. In the marching file of stately office buildings on Clive Street, now Netaji Subhas Road, and Dalhousie Square, or now BBD Bagh, the commercial hub of the city, featured predominant British names. Emblazoned on brass panels at imposing entrances were names like Andrew Yule, James Finlay, Duncan Bros, Macneill and Barry, Gillanders Arbuthnot, Bird & Co., Balmer Lawrie, etc. Many of these companies continued to be controlled from England but some had begun to be taken over by wealthy Marwaris. They, however, seemed to be happy to stay in the background, maintaining the labels and the trappings of yore, believing that they gave greater prestige to the company.

Presiding over these mammoth mercantile houses were the white burra sahibs who lived in gracious bungalows thoughtfully provided by their companies in the fashionable localities of Ballygunge and Alipore. The memsahibs could be even more imposing. An invitation to tea was an honour not to be lightly taken. Apart from the signal that the husband was in the good books of the company, it carried with it an implicit hint of an exalted role the wife was expected to play in the future. At four o'clock in the afternoon, the lavender-scented memsahib would emerge fresh from her siesta to preside over an exquisitely laid-out tea on a manicured lawn, while liveried servants scuttled in the shrubbery at her bidding, fetching trays of wafer-thin cucumber sandwiches and fruit cake made by the bavarchi in the kitchen. The young wife, rendered somewhat breathless by such august attentions, was meant to absorb the tradition and carry it forward when her turn came.

About this time we were allotted a company flat in the exclusive 4, Lord Sinha Road complex. Though it was on the second floor, the flat was large, with three spacious bedrooms that all opened onto a large hall in the centre, with a long kitchen at the far end. A metal spiral staircase from the kitchen led to the servants' quarters on the ground floor. The previous tenants had been a stylish avant garde couple who thought nothing of painting one wall, the ceiling and the fans of

The busy hum of social life in clubs portrayed by the cartoonist Mario Miranda.

the living room a muddy olive green. Another room was similarly painted in a deep grey. When the fans moved I thought of giant bats whirling in the air. We moved in with two beds, a Godrej almirah, a Regency dining table with eight chairs bought at an auction, a sideboard and a newly recruited raw-boned Nepali servant.

The furniture for the other rooms was being designed and assembled by my designer school-friend who had been originally sent to England by his father to study law but ended up doing interiors under Lord Mountbatten's son-in-law, the distinguished designer David Hicks. He designed a long sofa for the drawing room and covered it with superior jute cloth, the colour of raw silk. It looked very attractive but could be prickly to sit on. The friend also made an elegant wingchair, side tables and a coffee table, and persuaded us to buy an olive-green carpet to match the ceiling. Along with the flat came an air-conditioner and a generous allowance from the company to buy furniture, though the executive was expected to pay for the curtains and carpets.

The colonial buildings on Clive street Calcutta have stood the test of time.

The Royal Calcutta Golf club established in 1829. In the late 60's, the sun seemed not to have set on the Empire.

The Calcutta Club in the 1960s.

Andrew Yule, one of the oldest British companies in Calcutta.

My love affair with Curzon began in 1967 when I saw his statue being shifted from its lofty pedestal in front of the Victoria Memorial of Calcutta and relegated to the back. I was somewhat taken aback by the gleeful response of the Calcuttans to this act.

Lord Curzon, Viceroy of India (1899-1905), and Lady Mary Curzon, in the Peacock dress, which proved to be unlucky!

Curzon's statue was moved from its commanding presence at the front of Victoria Memorial, to be replaced by that of Aurobindo Ghosh, who lead the militant nationalistic movement against Partition.

The Viceroy on a state visit to Burdwan.

Government House, Calcutta, which derived its inspiration from Kedleston Hall, Curzon's family estate in Derbyshire.

CURZON AND I

My love affair with Curzon began in 1967 when I saw his statue being shifted from its lofty pedestal in front of the Victoria Memorial of Calcutta and relegated to the back. I was somewhat taken aback by the gleeful response of the Calcuttans to this act. I did not understand then, as I know more the full implication of the partition, aborted within six years, which not merely foreshadowed the demise of the Raj but also laid the foundation for Pakistan.

I first saw Calcutta as a bride in 1965, and was immediately struck by its imperial past. I longed to capture the certain *je ne sais quoi* of this glorious, anachronistic world now being washed into history. To me Calcutta in many ways seemed Curzon's city though he had left it after the disastrous termination of his viceroyalty, never to return. The city was very dear to him and he protested vehemently when the capital was shifted to Delhi. Curzon's presence lingers in Government House, a building modelled—by strange coincidence—on his ancestral home in Kedleston Hall in Derbyshire almost a century before he became Viceroy. He had inspired the Archaeological Survey of India and we owe a huge debt to him for restoring all that was beautiful in our heritage. He guided the building of the grandiloquent Victoria Memorial which floats in ethereal splendour over the vast, hot expanse of Calcutta's Maidan.

I felt the Viceroy deserved a requiem.

He had a fascinating life. Hailed as the future prime minister when still at Oxford, 39 year-old Curzon was handsome, brilliant and the youngest viceroy to be sent to India, his 28 year-old wife, the-first American spouse any viceroy had had. Queen Victoria had personally selected him, setting aside the claims of her son-in-law. It was like a journey to heaven. Yet six years later he returned home a broken man, his viceroyalty in shambles. What went wrong? My curiosity was aroused and I set out to explore.

Ignorant of this period in Indian history but agog with curiosity I had got myself attached to Professor Hiren Chakrabarti of Presidency College through a common friend. A man of great erudition, Prof. Chakrabarti had misgivings about my credentials. A middle-aged housewife, that too a "Company Wife" as we were known, was to him like Eliot's superficial creatures who "...come and go. Talking of Michelangelo."

Trying to shake me off, he made me read more than 40 books on the British period in India. By then I was properly hooked on the subject. Next step was England, where I had to spend weeks pouring over family archives in ancestral mansions with long draughty corridors. Curzon's family at Kedleston Hall were most welcoming as also Nigel Nicolson of Sissinghurst Castle who loaned me Lady Mary Curzon's original letters from India. They told an incredible tale. There was also Sir Anthony Glyn in Paris offering to tell me about his grandmother Eleanor Glyn's tempestuous love affair with Curzon. It had for me all the ingredients of a great historical drama.

My husband whose idea it was in the first place, would teasingly refer to Curzon as "the other man in my wife's life". My daughters had to put up with slapdash meals and neglected

With Curzon's descendants, Lord and Lady Scarsdale at Kedleston Hall.

homework as their mother went in search of Curzon. The odyssey took me seven years, ending in a biography and a doctorate from Calcutta University.

Curzon's attitude towards his family, about which he remained a compulsive myth-maker, was baffling. One of the brightest of students at Eton, he was pulled up for cheating in an examination. Yet he had the temerity to tell the students of Calcutta University in a Convocation speech that truth had taken a high place in the West before it was similarly honoured in the East!

To find the answers I probed the upper-class mid-Victorian England in which Curzon was born, the quirks of fate that made his father, a clergyman, inherit Kedleston Hall, before going on to touch an adolescence stained by a scandal resulting in the expulsion from Eton of the homosexual Master Oscar Browning.

I travelled over the green quadrangles of Kedleston, Eton, and Oxford where doting parents and friends had made Curzon feel he was a "very superior person", so superior that he always had to carry the burden of his admirers' ambitions.

In his adolescent years neither his parents nor his teachers nor his friends tried to protect him from the punitive anarchy of his overweening will. Early in life he had made the heady discovery that if there was resistance, he could ride roughshod over it and stride towards his chosen goal. It drove him into self-destructive corners from which there was no return.

Curzon has not been forgiven in India for his partition of Bengal. Though he made it out to be an administrative measure to relieve an overburdened province, Indian opinion has always taken the Viceroy's act, and rightly so, to be a Machiavellian measure to 'divide and rule' India by tearing apart the province on communal lines, giving birth to a Muslim majority province in the east.

The partition opened up a Pandora's box. Overnight nationalism and separatism began to strike hammer blows at the roots of British power and Indian unity, neither of which were consequences Curzon intended. The Raj was at its high noon at the commencement of his viceroyalty. Now dark clouds gathered to eclipse the sun!

Lord Curzon: the Last of the British Moghuls *was published by Oxford University Press in 1992.*

The expansive grounds of Keddleston Hall.

Nigel Nicholson of Sissinghurst Castle.

Sumptuous interiors of Kedleston Hall.

Stage actress Elinor Glynn, whom Curzon courted with a tiger skin!

GUEST ON HIRE

The Statesman, February 11, 1980

Our chief guest was one of those perfectly turned out burra sahebs whom I had not thought existed outside the book. A slender, distinguished-looking man with a permanently bored and slightly supercilious manner, his suits breathed of Saville Row. He played polo over weekends, went on Home Leave to England every summer and was the only human being I had come across who actually called his servants Koi Hai. His accent was pure BBC—measured, slow, patrician and, had we not known that he was a grammer school boy, it would be easy to mistake him for the younger son of an English Lord with vast ancestral estates and a stately home tucked away in Derbyshire.

Lord Mountbatten and the Maharaja of Jaipur. Hobnobbing with royalty was highly prized.

This worthy burra saheb was a valued client of the Company. We, still struggling on the lower rungs of the commercial ladder, were sternly told it was no small honour for us to be given the privilege of entertaining this august being in our home. Alas! We were also aware of the risk.

The menu had not posed as great a problem as choosing the other guests. Our client was known to be awfully fastidious about the people he dined with. It was then that a helpful friend suggested the Rear Admiral: that charmingly suave European gentleman, exuding masses of old world courtesy, who for some reason had taken up temporary residence in Calcutta just then.

My eyes brightened. A tall erect gentleman, the Rear Admiral wore a monocle over one eye and, in his after dinner conversation had generally let it be known that he was a retired naval man on excellent terms with everybody from the Mountbattens downwards. To us he became much more—a fairy godparent.

The evening had not begun well. The bearer, unfamiliar in his new coat, had bent so low over the tray of drinks as to knock a glass of whisky straight into the burra saheb's lap.

"Oh no!" I gasped.

"It does not matter," said the burra saheb, "we all make mistakes." A funereal silence had then descended upon the room with the burra saheb looking pointedly at the stains on his trousers.

A century dragged by before the bell rang again bringing in our Rear Admiral. He glided across the room to me, raised my two hands in his, fixed me a melting eye and said. "My dear! My dear! Will you ever forgive me? Oh! to be so late. The traffic! Such traffic!"

I smiled back, feeling all the world was a stage and I was right in the middle. "Do meet our guest," I said to the Rear Admiral.

"Delighted to," replied the Rear Admiral, stretching his arm in the direction of the burra saheb. Then, as though a thought had struck him, he fixed his monocle firmly, bent down to have a closer look, raised his head and pronounced, "But we've met before!"

"Have we?" said the burra saheb in his most disagreeable voice.

"But of course, old boy!" beamed the Rear Admiral, "at the Garden Party at Buckingham Palace. You remember?" The burra saheb looked suspicious. The Rear Admiral smiled back in his most affable manner.

"Or was it at that little dinner given by the Mountbattens?" continued the incorrigible Rear Admiral. "Let me think. Yes, that was it. Remember..? The Jaipurs were also there. And all that talk about polo?"

"Well," said our burra saheb, having found himself foisted with the reputation of a man who hobnobs with royalty, "Well, if you say so...." Then at last the burra saheb beamed widely.

THE LADY BUYS A SARI

The Times of India, June 14, 1964

"What new saris have you got today? A fresh stock of Kashmere silks? Oh no, much too common! Everyone wears them these days. Why, even my ayah has a Kashmere now. I want something absolutely new and different... Oh, raw silk? Yes, that blue one certainly looks gorgeous. Could I drape it on for a moment? Ah..! it does look grand. Goes so well with my colouring too, doesn't it? And the silver work is so attractive... so, so delicate and yet so bold. What price? Rs 570 for this? No, no, I don't think it's too expensive at all. Quite reasonable, really. Just a minute... don't make the bill yet... With me, as you well know, it is not a question of money, but simply one of taste. I always like to get something exclusive and not so loud and never care how much I have to spend on it....

"Do show me some of those batik prints... So, so original and uninhibited I am told... Oh, so these are the batiks? Very unusual... frankly, a little too unusual. Not that I am unfashionable really, but between you and me, I think I would get... what-do-you-call-it... a colour phobia? I just don't see how our women can bear to go around in these monstrosities. It's a craze for wanting to be different.

"Varieties in cottons, Chanderis? Oh dear no! My neighbour bought a Chanderi last month and after the first washing, mind you the very first washing, it went into shreds... By the way, my sister bought a cotton saree from your shop last year. Perhaps you remember it? No? I didn't think you would... It was quite pretty really. It was pink in colour and had little peacocks all over the pallav. I would have loved to buy one just like that.

"Perhaps you better show me some dacrons? Can they be washed at home? Good. What about the ironing? None at all? Tell me, are society women wearing it this year? Yes? Oh, but it would be a little uncomfortable to wear in the hot weather, wouldn't it? Yes, I know I said I wanted something very fashionable and new... but it must be comfortable to wear. The texture of the material never bothers me so long as it is not thick. On the other hand, I'd hate to be seen around in a flimsy affair. The colour? As you know I never fuss so long as it is pale but not dowdy.

"Surely, you understand what I am looking for. After all, your shop is supposed to sell sarees to suit all tastes. Such a pity you don't seem to have anything I care for. I was so looking forward to buying at least half a dozen saris today.

In mid-1971, there were harrowing tales of refugees fleeing from East Pakistan during the war for Bangladesh.

REFUGEES SPEAK: 1971

The Illustrated Weekly of India, July 25, 1971

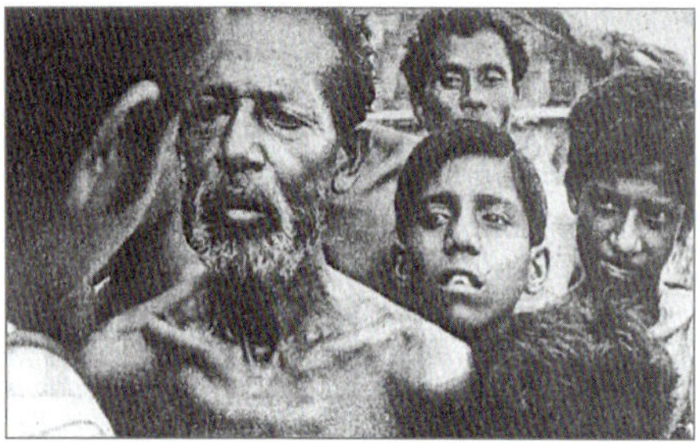

Death in Sahara Camp

Kali Devi, a weary, coy-eyed maid of 25, sat back upon her haunches at the relief centre office picking lice from her five year-old son's sore-infested head. The doctor in charge told us that she had come in to announce the death of her husband. She waited for the corpse to be taken away.

Kali Devi is stricken with a strange passive resignation. Tucked in at her waist is a ration card. Before returning to her tent she must collect her quota of rice and dal. The dead are gone, the living must be fed.

One dark night a month ago a posse of trigger-happy Pakistani soldiers came down on their village. Kali, her husband, her brother and her child fled across to the border and to safety. They abandoned their two bighas of land and parents too old to travel.

Kali's husband is now dead. "A cholera victim," the doctor mechanically says. Her brother is running high fever. "He too may soon die." On the road outside stands a little van: it is for the disposal of the dead. Kali's husband is dumped inside. The van waits to fill up its total cargo of three corpses before it can make its trip to the burning ghat. "It should not take more than two or three hours," says the doctor.

Salt Lake Encampment

At Salt Lake camp on the outskirts of Calcutta, Manohar Rai and his family sat apart from the rabble as though conscious of their superior status.

Manohar has left behind 120 bigbas (40 acres) of land in his native village of Dumuria in Khulna: a landlord of standing a month ago whom an unkind shift in history has reduced to a serf. Nevertheless he is quite clear that he would not like to return. "My land has been given away to Bihari Muslims. What is there to return to?"

In strange variance with Renubala, his plump, comely, double-chinned wife, is their one-month-old, shrunken child. Cruel blue veins are etched out in his tiny, baby skull and desolate eyes stare out hauntingly—a corpse gasping for life. Greedy flies are settling on his face.

All day the family sits in the shade of a wall of an unfinished building. At night, they creep into an empty drainpipe to sleep. Being newcomers to the camp there is no room for them in the tents.

A stone's throw away is a naked little urchin, thin and reedy, licking his curry-stained fingers with puckish relish. He is a homeless waif who was separated from his parents and washed onto the shores of Salt Lake among the wreck of Bangladesh.

Mandalpara Camp

Renubala and Manohar have lost only their home and their status. But grey-haired toothless Sarala Devi whom we met at the Mandalpara camp near Bongaon has seen her grown-up son, Anil, being mown down by sten-gun fire. "Those Punjabi soldiers murdered my son," she wailed in an unconsolable frenzy.

Anil's neighbour, Gopalchandra Pal, also a tile mason by profession, thought himself lucky. He had run away into the fields and avoided the firing squad. But he was not destined to escape. A soldier caught up with him and deftly drove a bayonet through his ribs. His inconsolable, weeping wife told us his tale.

"Three refugee families are staying in an outhouse on my land," says a chaiwala. "I have loaned it to them. After all they are our brethren."

Not everyone shares the chaiwala's magnanimity. A letter-writer in a leading Calcutta daily asks in alarm: "Today they live on our doorsteps. What is going to stop them from moving into our homes tomorrow?"

We saw refugees lodged on verandahs. Every bit of high level land on the wayside has been annexed by little shelters of bamboo and thatched coconut palm.

Men, women and children are flooding the border-side towns like swarms of locusts. Bongaon, on a week day, looks like a Sunday market town with aimless crowds milling around like teeming maggots in a corpse. The government relief centres, besides providing a ration of rice, dal, vegetables, fuel and cooking oil, give 25 to 50 paise a day to each refugee. This has brought out the quaking fly-covered confections, the pink and orange sherbets, biscuits, bidis, brightly coloured wooden toys, the dust and the germs. Prices are spiralling upward, beyond the means of the common man who will soon begin blaming the refugees for his plight.

Snehlata Nundi and her old father-in-law owe their lives to their Muslim neighbours. Snehlata, a dour, plain woman of 28 with heavy features and pimply cheeks had squinted hopefully at me. Her home was in Faridpur. Her husband had gone underground at the advance of Yahya Khan's army. Their Muslim neighbours feigned allegiance to the Yahya regime and hid her in their home. When the all-clear signal was given she had fled to the border.

Nirmal Hriday in Calcutta was an unique institution that ensured "a beautiful death for people who lived wretched lives to die like angels—loved and wanted".

Nirmal Hriday, or the Home for the Sick & Dying Destitutes near Kalighat in South Calcutta.

The men's ward at Nirmal Hriday.

NIRMAL HRIDAY: A HOME FOR THE DYING

Imprint, September 1978

Mother Teresa comforting the women at Nirmal Hriday

NEAR THE KALI TEMPLE in south Calcutta is a unique institution called Nirmal Hriday—Home for Destitutes, Dying. All around you, as you stand in one of its two spacious dormitories, you will see a marching file of low-framed beds, clinging to the walls' edges. On them lie a long huddle of shrunken shrivelled humans with ghoulish smudges for eyes: corpses before they are dead. It is not at first sight an exuberant scene. The air is grim with the odour of death. But by a strange paradox, there is none of that cold forlornness of abandonment here.

If you are lucky, you may spot among the saree-clad nuns a luminous presence—Mother Teresa herself. Brisk and methodical, she goes from patient to patient, sometimes stopping to listen to a hysterical plea: washing a gangrene here, helping to give a morphine injection there. Sometimes, she kneels down to pray and to gently shut the eyes of a corpse staring vacantly into space. Her very presence has an indescribable effect on the inmates. These people, gasping for life gaze at her with a rapt, heart-rending confidence as though her touch, like a wand of magic, will dispel all their lonely misery.

The inspiration behind this institution came one day in 1948 when Mother saw a female patient lying on a pavement in front of a Calcutta hospital, maggots crawling over her body. The hospital authorities had no place for her. Mother Teresa sat on the street with the dying woman all through the night. It was a long, desolate vigil and, while sharing it, the victim's utter sense of loneliness communicated itself to her. With it came a realisation—almost a revelation, that life holds no greater tragedy than the chill of abandonment. This is an ailment which no hospital can heal, no medicine can cure, no surgery separate, no drug relieve: neither the ancient wisdom of the East nor the modern affluence of the West has an answer for this.

In 1952, the Calcutta Corporation handed over an old dharamsala near the Kali temple to Mother Teresa which she converted into a home for the dying. At first, the Brahmin priests raised Cain. They felt that the atmosphere had been defiled. Ironically today, Mother Teresa is accepted as an incarnation of 'Ma' herself, by the very same temple priests.

Soon after our marriage, we were sent off on a short posting to Fort Cochin. We were assigned the upper half of a bungalow which we shared with a British colleague. Richard had a bevy of domestics. Verghese, our first and only recruit seemed a veritable Jeeves.

The Beach Bungalow in Fort Cochin which we acquired later, was probably built in 1890s, and is listed as a heritage property today.

A JEEVES IN THE HOUSE

WHEN I ARRIVED TO set up my first household in Fort Cochin, I had vaguely assumed that servants would only play a small role in our domestic harmony. I had fantasies fully developed by glossy women's weeklies of being the perfect housewife, always gay and debonaire, never a harassed moment, never complaining; ready to welcome the weary breadwinner in the evening to an exquisitely tidy home sweet home where a servant would be waiting, eager to answer summons. I was a bride then and under the anaesthesia of newly-wedded bliss.

Fort Cochin encouraged this belief. There is a *savoir faire* of the ancient regime about the place perpetuated by soft-footed, salaaming servants fussing around with an outdated protocol.

Verghese, our first recruit, did seem a veritable Jeeves. With his stiff carriage and slightly supercilious air he gave the impression of a man who could handle any situation with aplomb.

It was we who disappointed him. A cook-bearer was an anachronism in his vocabulary. Apparently he and his ancestors had served in the days of pukka sahebs in whose households they had lorded over a small but complete army of servants. Now he viewed with dismay the prospect of manual labour. Pukka sahebs were no longer plentifully around and Verghese was a realist. He reconciled himself to working for us But grudgingly, only for our sake. He gave us the feeling that he was obliging us, helping us tide over a difficulty.

Verghese soon took possession of our home and our lives, smothering us with elaborate and embarrassing courtesy. Our activities were stiffened by etiquette: we were not allowed to get out of bed before seven when Verghese brought in the morning tea and drew the curtains, my husband was not permitted a bath unless Verghese first ran the water. Verghese did not insist on the Somerset Maugham ritual of our dressing for dinner, nevertheless, like a ceremonial high priest he would preside over the proceedings from the background.

There were many squeamish p's and q's of social behaviour with which Verghese acquainted me. Once when I asked for badminton nets to be put up in the garden Verghese squirmed as though his deepest sensibilities had been offended. "Madam," he sternly informed me, "badminton only play in winter." I was being the parvenu again.

Verghese was an excellent cook and at his best at a party. Like an excited child he would burst into baritone hummings as he darted here and there to lay out a gourmet's orgy. He would consult me about the menu, but only perfunctorily.

"What sweetdish you wanting?" he would sternly ask. Without giving me a moment to think, "Finis," he would cry, as though impatient at my indecision, "Finis. I give marines pudding."

I shuddered with silent horror but had not the courage to ask. Marines turned out to be a meringue pie, the most delectable that we had eaten.

Verghese left us abruptly to work for a bachelor at twenty rupees less per month. "But why Verghese?" I wailed feeling betrayed. For all his authoritarianism, we were beginning to develop a liking for him and I had thought it was mutual.

Verghese blushed. He looked down at his frail feet and shuffled them uncomfortably. It was the marketing, he finally explained.

"But I pay you so much more by way of wages," I coaxed as I had been doing the household purchasing.

"Yes, yes, madam," he agreed soothingly. "But the dastur!" he sighed. With no marketing to handle, there was no haggling, no fun of making that extra rupee.

Mani was a smooth and zesty little grandmother with a shrewd eye on the world around her. She next came to work for us as my husband was often called away on tour and it would be nice to have a woman around the house. Besides, as she was old there is no likelihood of romantic complications with the other servants, my husband hopefully said.

But we were wrong. Mani had her amours. Both the mali and the driver vied for her questionable charms. We soon found our household vicariously involved in the emotional entanglements of a *menage a trois*. We lived in perpetual tension of murder taking place in our backyard. But Mani artfully kept the players apart.

Mani was well-versed with the old wives' tale that the best way to a man's heart is through his stomach. So she plied her beaus with food. Overnight I found that large stocks of flour, butter and sugar would disappear from the pantry. When it happened once too often I went into a fitful rage and shouted, "This is the limit Mani! Next time you will have to go."

Mani promptly burst into a flood of tears, seeming inconsolable in her repentance. "Madam, Mani too much bad. You say go and I go. You say stay and I stay. You my Lord and Master. I got nobody." Mani stayed. But her being all alone in this world was not strictly true.

"Suddenly my mother dead, my mother very antique!" she told me one morning. I quickly dispatched her with a generous amount to cover the funeral expenses. Over the months I was to learn that Mani had a disturbingly large battalion of sick and needy relatives all solely dependent upon her for time, money, old clothes and sympathy. Once when Mani returned after a week's disappearance I asked with heavy sarcasm, "Who was it this time now Mani? Not your mother again, I hope."

"Yes, madam. Just like my mother only," Mani said wiping a fictitious tear.

And over the last years we have survived many more of their tribe. All in all our domestic acquisitions have been a tolerant and a friendly lot. One was collecting credit in our name from the shops in the neighbourhood, a detail which came to our notice soon after his departure; another who prided himself on his looks—he was handsome in a Dilip Kumar sort of a way—spent all his mornings writing elaborate applications to film producers in Bombay while he should have been dusting and polishing; a third thought that our new hi-fi set was purchased solely for his entertainment; yet another quietly locked the kitchen door and went off for the evening when my husband was bringing important business clients home to dinner. But we survived.

A watercolour of Fort Cochin painted in 1800.

AT YOUR SERVICE

The Statesman, May 26, 1978

I WAS A NEW BRIDE then busy setting up my first house in Fort Cochin. I was therefore, considerably flattered to receive in the mail one day a heavy white envelope emblazoned with arms and insignia and hand-addressed to me. Inside was a charmingly personal letter from the Managing Director of a new department store in a nearby metropolis.

In tones of old world courtesy, the good gentleman, welcoming me to my new abode, wished me a long and happy married life and proceeded to catalogue for me an array of worldly goods I would need to ensure domestic harmony. Getting more business-like, he told me that on the subject of furniture they had all the staples like sofas, beds, dining tables, dressing tables, the lot. But if I wished to supplement these standard ready-mades with period furniture, I could do so by glancing through a catalogue from their Ye Olde Curiosity Shop. One month's notice was necessary, he warned, which was not too much time for reproducing a genuine antique. All I had to do was tick off my preference on the enclosed business reply card.

This of course, was only a small sample of their services: the corporation's motto being "The Difficult we supply right away, the Impossible takes us a little longer". The letter ended vowing undying devotion and super-efficient computerised service. What more could I ask?

Alas! our budget could not stretch to more than a couple of the tantalising 'Thousand Creature Comforts' mentioned by my good friend. I, therefore, settled for a green plastic bucket which I did not really need.

A week later I was considerably alarmed to receive a reply thanking me for my order for an automatic washing machine, regretting that at present stocks were exhausted and assuring delivery at the first possible date. Obviously the computerised service had gone haywire, mixing up my order with someone else's.

I promptly wrote off pointing out the error. But too late! The very next morning we were woken up by a delivery man. He had the grave face of an undertaker and was dressed in a black tunic with gold braid. On the road outside was a large black van resembling a hearse.

"Your order," he said to us in the tragic tones of one addressing someone recently bereaved. Our protests fell on deaf ears. "My orders are orders," said he sanctimoniously. "If you have complaints, you can make them to the corporation."

We did. The correspondence extended over three years. The last reply from the Board of Directors read:

Dear Madam,

We are in receipt of your letter of March 2, 1969. In communicating in future, kindly indicate your reference number, complaint number, file number, nationality, number of children, occupation and hobbies.

We are happy to inform you that your complaint has been put before the Board. Its decision will be intimated to you.

In the meanwhile we enclose our new catalogue on marble bathtubs. In anticipation of your esteemed order, we remain,

Yours faithfully.

THE WEARY-GO-ROUND

The Times of India, April 19, 1967

THE FLAT WE HAD JUST moved into was beautifully furnished, just like something one is constantly seeing in glossy American *Better Homes* magazines. But having taken a recent three-month course in interior decoration, I was inclined to be fussy. A certain *je ne sais quoi* was missing I decided.

After much debate, I settled upon the living room light. The existing set-up was woefully outdated. It had to be replaced.

The electricians were most co-operative. Certainly madam, they smoothly assured me on the telephone, their men were fully equipped to handle the most exacting of jobs. I need give it not a single thought.

Manohar was an enormous hairy ape with hands like a pair of spades, "What type light you are wanting? Americaine, English or Paris?" he asked in gnarled English, thrusting into my hands a curry-stained magazine cutting to better illustrate his point.

The American was a big, bold cartwheel of light, all brass and chromium plated, while the English was a sedate little lamp with a prim Victorian shade; the French was more romantically inclined, with an intricately carved bracket and black satin-shade—it cast in effect no light at all. "Finis," interrupted Manohar, tired of my indecision, "I give best job."

He then produced some wire and an ancient hook that could have well served the crooked captain on Treasure Island and proceeded to work upon the ceiling. Eventually fixing the hook, Manohar swung his massive frame on it.

Just to demonstrate its strength, he proudly explained to me. Down came the hook with Manohar clinging to it for dear life, and with them, a great part of the ceiling itself.

For a long moment Manohar gazed at the gaping hole above in sad puzzlement and dismay. Then, in hushed confidence he leaned over and assured me, "madam need not worry". He happened to have a handy carpenter in his family who would put humpty-dumpty together again for just 100 rupees.

Next morning the door bell rang at six. My husband opened the door to a small, sallow youth of about 16, armed with a hatchet and a crow-bar. "Number two, is it?" the intruder demanded.

"Er... yes," replied my husband, unwilling to commit himself.

"Well then," he announced, "I am Govind, the nephew of the Manohar."

"What is it?" I called over the bannisters heavy-eyed with sleep.

"Govind," said my husband guardedly.

Govind eyed me suspiciously. I became conscious of my old nightie. The print was faded and the colour never suited me.

"Okay," said Govind shuffling past me. "Where are the ceilings?"

I had misgivings about Govind.

It was not his technical know-how that I doubted. It was his height. Govind was four feet two and could not reach the low ceiling standing on a stool on top of our highest table and had to send a servant across the road to get a ladder, and my husband after him to tell him which size he wanted. I acted as a sort of a mate handing him tools and things.

After this went on for a few days, my husband took to coming home early so that he could hold the ladder while I went down on all fours to pick up the nails which Govind seemed to be constantly dropping on the floor.

Before the month was out, work on the ceiling was completed. Govind left us with a generous share of his grimy fingerprints on our walls and a cheerful promise to send a brother-in-law to paint them off.

Thus came Shrikant into our home. A squint-eyed little man with slightly squashed ears which did not match, Shrikant confided to me in a moment of bonhomie that he was considered among the foremost abstract artists of the generation, but abstract artists being cheaper by the dozen, he was forced to spend his mornings painting walls. He bore his cross cheerily.

"Can you get the exact shade of grey?" I asked nervously.

"Ya sure," he replied, He mixed several colours on a palate and smeared the mixture on the wall. He then turned to me with a smile.

"But this is purple," I cried in horror.

"Ya sure," he replied obligingly. He mixed again. In a spurt of enthusiasm he threw in several more colours. By the end of the day the room was painted a bright shade of violet.

Accustomed to his predecessors, I had marked Shrikant out as a potential begetter of work. I had waited like a coiled spring ready for the weary-go-round to begin once again. The beds could have collapsed or the bathroom pipes obligingly burst so that his entire fraternity could invade my house. But nothing happened. Not for a whole week anyway.

On the eighth day a young man fancifully clad in a scarlet satin shirt with bold ochre stripes and a pair of tight leathery pants rang the bell. No sooner the door was opened than in quick furtive movements he wedged himself inside. A mop of crisp unruly curls covered his ears and most of his eyes. I was considerably alarmed.

Recovering his poise the hairy apparition condescendingly waved a ringed hand at what had once been my home-sweet-home and said the flat was basically good. Just as his cousin-brother Shrikant had told him.

The furniture was tolerable. He smiled encouragingly. But the colours?

Why for the sombre greys and blues? "They for old peoples," he said.

What I needed, he said, was some brightening. A rani pink here and a parrot green there. It was all the rage he assured me. Why, all the film-wallahs were doing it. And now, was it just not my good fortune, he smiled,that he was an interior decorator and just the right man for the job?

An Indian Express story by Vishnu Varma on September 10, 2019 says, "Today the population of white Jews has whittled down to less than ten in Cochin. A popular resident, Sarah Jacob Cohen passed away last a week at age 96."

The elaborate and well-preserved interior of the Jewish Synagogue at Fort Cochin.

THE PARADESI SYNAGOGUE

The Illustrated Weekly of India, March 2, 1969

IN THE GROUNDS of the Maharaja of Cochin's palace and overlooking a Hindu shrine stands the Paradesi Synagogue. This close proximity to a princely dwelling symbolises the goodwill the Jews have enjoyed in Kerala through the ages.

The Synagogue completed 400 years last December and, at the invitation of the 87+ member Jewish community of Cochin, the Prime Minister Mrs Indira Gandhi visited Kerala to inaugurate the celebrations to mark the occasion. A 20-paise commemorative stamp was issued by the postal department.

Stepping into the tranquillity of the Paradesi Synagogue, with its exquisite Chinese tiles and gleaming brass pulpit, one is filled with emotion as one thinks of these remarkable people who have preserved in this spot rituals and relics almost as old as time.

The Paradesi Synagogue is perhaps in some ways a microcosm of the entire Jewish experience. It epitomises the history of the Jews in Kerala, a history which, in spite of the unfailing hospitality of the local rajas, has by no means been unchequered and which, to an extent has been a re-enactment in miniature of the fate of the Jews the world over. But if the Jews in Kerala have suffered, they have done so only at the hands of foreigners.

Ostracised and excommunicated, haunted and hounded the world over, the Jews are known to have been received in Malabar, in their own words, with "a liberality that can scarcely be understood". Driven from their natural home in Judaea after the destruction of Jerusalem by the Romans, some 10,000 Jews in A.D. 70 sought refuge in the port of Cranganore or Shingly as it was then called. This was followed by mass immigration of about 75,000 men, women and children in A.D. 370. The reputation of this lush coast as a haven of refuge for the dispersed Jews soon spread to Europe. Centuries later, when the Jews of Spain fell prey to the conquistadors, at the time of the Inquisition in 1492, they instinctively set sail for Malabar. Not merely did the local princes give them food and shelter, they made them grants and such privileges as accorded only to the highest of Nair chieftains.

The most famous of these grants, made in A.D. 379 by King Ravivarman, is recorded on a pair of copper plates and preserved to this day in the Synagogue. It tells of the handing over of the rights of the village of Anjuvannam to the Jewish leader Joseph Rabban as a hereditary possession "so long as the world and moon exist".

Until the 15th century the Jews flourished in peace and plenty in their little settlement at Shingly, absorbing themselves in the life of the local community as merchants and financiers, landowners and astute courtiers, but zealously retaining their racial and religious individuality.

The fame of Shingly spread far and wide. Rabi Nissim, the Hebrew poet and traveller, sang in the 14th century:

I travelled from Spain
I had heard of the city of Shingly
I longed to see an Israel King
Him, I saw with my own eyes.

But, alas, the Jewish state of Anjuvannam was not to survive as long as the world and the moon. With an abrupt end of the Rabban dynasty and in the ensuing confusion, further chaos was added by a volatile dispute with the Moors over the highly competitive pepper trade. Sparks kindled into a blazing fire as the Moors led an attack upon the Jews, sacking their homes and synagogues in a devastation which has been compared with the destruction of Jerusalem.

The fleeing Jews found sanctuary with the Maharaja of Cochin. He set apart a portion of his own palace grounds for them. There they built the Jew Town in 1567 and the Paradesi Synagogue in 1568. Thus from the ashes of the old arose the new.

The epic of toil and tears was however not yet over. For 160 years the Portuguese made savage and satanic inroads into their lives, coming down like wolves on peaceful ghettos, destroying homes and burning the Synagogue. But the will to survive ran high in the Jewish blood. Thrown out of their homes and barred from trade, deprived of a common place for worship, they tenaciously clung to one another, preserving through the darkest days their oldest relics and traditions.

Their patience was rewarded after the advent of the Dutch. From that time to the present day they have lived in peace. They became big merchants, their ships sailed from Arabia to far Cathay. The renewed prosperity was quickly reflected in the Paradesi Synagogue. Ezechiel Rahabi, an eminent Jew, brought 400 willow patterned tiles, no two identical, from China in the year 1760 to embellish the Synagogue. In the same year he added to the Synagogue a square clock tower with dials in Hebrew, Malayalam and Roman.

The passing years saw the construction of a beautifully gilded and carved ark to contain the Torah scrolls. Water was considered too ordinary for mixing its mortar, hence coconut milk was used! Gleaming silver cases were made for the Torah and golden crowns to cover them. In 1805 the Maharaja of Travancore presented one of his crowns to the Synagogue.

Over the centuries, the Jews have fully matched the local hospitality by their unflinching loyalty and liberal contribution to the life of their adopted home. Their role in adding to the material well-being of Malabar hardly needs emphasis: they even performed military service for the rajas. On one occasion, in 1550, a battle had to be postponed because Jewish soldiers were reluctant to fight on Sabbath day!

In the Dutch era, the Rahabi family played an important role in Cochin. Though they did not wield direct political power, they are known to have had an influence on the lives of many a member of the royal family.

When Hyder Ali threatened to attack Cochin in 1766, Ezechiel Rahabi sent three of his sons with rare spices, precious gems and soothing words to the court of the Muslim ruler. Appeased, Hyder turned his eyes to Canara. Even today the descendants of the Rahabis are prominent members of society in Cochin and make useful contribution to its life as doctors and lawyers and businessmen.

Most of the Jews of Cochin live in Jew Town. Should you make a journey down its single narrow street flanked by a file of uniformly squat whitewashed houses leading to the Synagogue, shades of Jerusalem will flash upon the inward eye. An old man with an embroidered cap and Semitic profile sits at a window upstairs gazing down on a knot of blue-eyed girls playing hopscotch. Occasionally a pair of small boys can be seen walking hand in hand, one carrying a dish of mutton patties for his aunt living further upstreet. Chattering voices are constantly heard tossed across the street in gay bonhomie. Everyone knows everyone else; everyone is related to everyone else and they all live together as one large family.

The family, however, has dwindled over the years. Twenty-five years ago there were some 1,500 Jews in and around Cochin. Today only 300 remain of whom 87 live in Cochin itself. The birth of Israel has drawn more and more of them to their ancient home. They migrate not because they are loved less in Cochin but because they love their Holy Land more.

It is perhaps too much to hope that the Jews will stay on in Cochin to celebrate the fifth centenary of the Paradesi Synagogue. But the Synagogue will endure as a lasting monument to the followers of Moses who came to Malabar and made it their home for two millenniums.

The whitewashed walls of the Synagogue. Note the beautiful clock on the tower.

GOD'S MEN AND GOD'S CHILDREN

On a holiday in Puri, we embarked on a cycle rickshaw excursion to the Jagannath temple in the old city. As soon as our vehicle turned onto the main square leading to the temple a horde of dhoti-clad priests descended upon us, like the Assyrians, as wolves on the fold. Shrieking pandas surrounded us, all anxious for our salvation.

The crowd grew to alarming proportions when suddenly, an old, toothless panda with a concave chest and a surprising amount of strength for his fragile appearance, elbowed his way to the forefront. He briskly took charge, pushing aside the others. "This way, this way," he commanded our rickshaw pullers, frowning like a man who has little time to waste. One young panda protested, but the old priest gave him a withering look. "Off with you, you country bumpkin! Can't you see that these town folks are my customers. Every year they come to Puri and every year I take them to the temple," he said without batting an eyelid.

Before I could protest at this gross untruth, our mentor turned to me and sternly ordered, "put out your right hand!" He quickly slapped a leaf on it, scooped two flowers on top and sprinkled them with a fistful of water from a container he held in one hand. "Come, you are ready for a darshan."

My husband decided it was time to intervene. Politely but firmly he said, "Thank you, but we would rather go to the temple on our own."

"Even our shastras say that it is the priest who can lead a man to God," he volunteered desperately. "Thank you," said my husband beginning to look very rebellious, "we would still rather do without you."

"You are Hindus?" he asked with sudden suspicion. When assured that we were, he said coaxingly, surely we would not like to miss an opportunity of visiting the inner temple? Coming closer, he whispered, "I know the inner priest. For ten rupees he will tell a special prayer. It will guarantee a place for you in heaven!"

We had no answer. "All right," said our priest like one concluding an important negotiation, "give eight rupees only. I will take care of everything. Just tell me your caste."

By now the gallery of idle spectators had grown considerably. But my husband had got the opportunity he was waiting for. Drawing himself up and in all solemnity, he said to the priest "Our caste, you asked? Well, if you must know, we are Hari-ke-jan."

The announcement had the desired, electrifying effect. The panda let go his hold over our vehicle as though he was scalded. The crowds beat an unholy retreat, with people falling hugger-mugger upon one another. Cries of *shantam papam* rent the air.

Unhindered, unimpeded we walked into the temple to bow to the Almighty. May He forgive us our aberration. Even Prince Yudhishthira in the *Mahabharata* had occasion to resort to a white lie. We are but frail mortals.

A visit to Goa before the backwash of modernity found a charming oasis of sun, sand and palm trees, where the East merged delightfully with the West.

The ferry across the Zuari brought to life by the Goan artist Mario Miranda.

DOWN AND OUT IN PANJIM

The Sunday Statesman, August 1, 1965

THE LUXURY TOURIST bus that took us to Panjim left Poona punctually at 6.30 a.m. and for the next fourteen hours roared steadily southward. With each mile, urbanisation with its skyline of chimneys, jagged sounds and industrial smoke seemed more and more remote and had less and less to do with the unchanging landscape.

Here was a family of water buffaloes drowsing in a pool of mud, now an acre of paddy waving and hectic as in a Van Gogh painting, a village of baked mud houses stewing in the noonday sun, a hoary old man indolent on a stringed cot puffing out great big rings of smoke.

The bus was specially designed for tourists but we seemed to be the only ones. Its only concession to luxury was a set of lurid red curtains designed not so much for the physical comfort of its passengers as to deceive the vigilant eye of the traffic inspector who may have viewed with disquiet the overcrowding within.

The driver was an obliging little fellow who used the bus for many a philanthropic detour. Scheduled halts on the route were few and far between, but he would stop every time a prosperous looking country gentleman on the road beckoned for a ride. This *tour de force* of a couple of miles for a rupee or two hardly mattered. The driver got some extra cash, the other passengers a fuller value for their money, and no one was any the poorer in the bargain.

Between hairpin bends when the bus seemed to roar above the ground he would turn to us happily to share the joy of his exhilarating driving. All day we sat through the drive, silent, rigid creatures, sending up fervent prayers hoping to get to our destination safely. At sunset, with the fertile plains left far behind, a curious salty tang tinged the air. In the distance a river swept by, and beyond, silhouetted against a giant hill of earth was Panjim.

There was no bridge across the Mandovi river. Everyone had to take the ferry. A businessman sat in a grey Mercedes masked in his glossy magazine, his car surrounded by a bevy of fat rollicking fisherwomen with mouths full of garlic and gold teeth, cluttering up the decks with their strong-smelling baskets. In a corner were a pair of wholly engrossed lovers, oblivious of speculative glances; in another, a village barber who gave a sly nudge to his friend as they watched with unabashed interest the intertwined couple.

All round us, as we disembarked from the ferry, was the city—wide, spacious, palm-lined avenues, and cramped terrace houses with apologetic gardens that scattered over the city and gingerly crept over the hillside a dull whitewash everywhere, the patina of trim respectability.

It was at the same time both old and new. One could see the mingling of East and West in the life around us; in the baroque churches where a kindly padre listened to a Konkani Brahmin's tale of woe, in the music and eating habits, in the pious Catholic who would not drive away the stray cow nibbling at his prize zinnias.

From the heart of town a road took us down south, a road now clinging perilously to the coast, now peering over sun-baked paddy fields, for a while stopping at Gaspar Dias, next to benches and playpens for frail old men and little girls in pink frocks. Along it the water whispered in continuous melody, a placid barge lumbering aimlessly. But the road soon rushes off, to the headland of Dona Paula, from where, across the waters and over a file of ship funnels, are the stark, smoke-filled towns of Vasco da Gama and Marmagao, industrial centres of Goa.

To the devout or to the camera-armed tourist Panjim has much to offer by way of temples and churches, each more memorable than the other. But for those who seek organised pleasure there is little. The backwash of modernity felt so insistently in cities like Bombay is conspicuous only by its absence. It is in the Municipal Gardens that the townsfolk assemble every evening to walk and talk; there are few shops, fewer cinemas, little of that irrepressible urge to get ahead; there is contentment and placidness.

Popular entertainment for the local gentry lies in periodic balls in hotels and clubs tucked away in far corners of the city. On these occasions the pattern of society so precisely etched on the canvas of Goa life and the forms of behaviour so generally accepted, fade as patrician and plebeian join hands to dance to the sagging melodies of Roman Rodrigues and his Zesty Band.

But for us it was just enough to be there. The sands of the beaches, dewy white and dappled light, stretched from here to eternity. Somewhere crouched in declivity was a thatch-roofed pub cared for by a fusty old man whose stock had grown old and mellow along with his own mature years. There was no juke-box jangle to accompany you. Only the lisping of tiny white crested wavelets as they romped on the shore. Over and beyond, swept by the azure skies, were the hills where wild flowers bloomed.

Tourist buses of yore!

A PALACE IN THE SKIES

The Statesman, December 21, 1977

Airlines the world over have entered some sort of an aeronautical Olympics, vying with one another to lure clients. Each one offers blandishments more beguiling than the next; in the few hours of flying time they promise to transport their passengers into a palace in the skies. The result is that anyone picking up a travel brochure is seized with Hamlet-like agonies on the airline to choose.

The glossy brochures, relentlessly circulated by travel agents, tantalise like the siren's call. Exotic international cuisine, wines, in-flight films, multi-channel stereo music, magazines and newspapers in various languages, Kleenex tissues, drawing crayons for children, nappies for babies and a multitude of cabin attendants are now basic essentials on all flights. Of course, in the First Class, the profusion of attendants is greater: probably they wait poised on their toes ready to run errands. The latest plane in the race even promises to lure you into space at the speed of sound: from London to Washington D.C. in time for the next meal.

To my wonder and indigestion, others offer old-world charm and a nine-course meal during a one-hour flight. On a London-Paris flight, no sooner were we airborne than the whole place became a gastronomic orgy. The airline seemed honour-bound to serve an elaborate meal with three different types of wines. We, in turn, felt obliged to gulp down everything in sight.

Hotel reservations? Why not let their man-on-the-spot do the job for us? We did and found ourselves ensconced in Hotel de la Roma in Paris, the airline's idea of a quiet hotel in a back street. Mundane details like bills had been left delightfully vague. We spent our holiday on the wrought-iron balcony, drinking cups at *cafe au lait*. There was little money left for anything else.

One airline specialises in business travel and offers secretarial services and a reference library on flight. Am I a globe-trotting tycoon, asks their brochure, negotiating multi-million dollar oil deals with the Sheikh of Araby? Or a contractor busy flinging bridges over the mighty Amazon? If so, few sleepers are available in the First Class, by prior reservation only. What, continues the brochure, is more important than a good night's sleep, provided you do not mind paying the price of building a miniature Taj Mahal? Monogrammed sheets and slippers are also available, but at three days' notice. Otherwise, I must make do with the airline's standard linen.

Meanwhile, my personal assistant will be relaxing in a stretch-out, deep-cushion chair in the Tourist Class. He will, however, have to reconcile himself to 'nine-abreast' seating, a film-show at a nominal charge and newspapers in just two languages. Most airlines now boast a bar on board with comely maidens with fluorescent green eyelids popping off champagne corks at the wave of a finger. Thoughtfully, this indulgence is reserved for its more sybaritic First Class customers. Music is provided in plenty, but alas! only on tape. No airline yet boasts of a live Hungarian violinist as he serenades his customers to sentimental Viennese melodies full of heart-throbbing glissandos and vibratos. Just a question of time?

LUNCH WITH MELISANDE

The Statesman, December 12, 1977

My friend Melisande had just converted her elegant Kensington home with its exquisitely chic French Edwardian aura into a functional, utilitarian, gadget-fitted apartment. I remarked on the change when I went to lunch with her on my last visit to London. "No, no. It's not a fad this time!" she protested.

Giddy aftermath of a Cambridge May ball!

Having known Melisande through giddy college days, I refrained from further comment. Melisande had married into one of those rare and almost extinct titled and monied British families; the ancestral stately home was neither sold, mortgaged, nor up on daily view for 30B. But alas! Melisande was now tired of flitting away her days as a pampered ornament of a lavish home.

"You don't know how much I've longed to get away from it all!" she cried passionately, fixing me with her irresistible, forget-me-not blue eyes. She had sacked her maids as a protest against the crass vulgarity of rich living. Her husband Algernon and she now only wanted to be able to run their home on their own. "How can I possibly explain to you that fierce ecstasy in a do-it-yourself joy?"

I had my own misgivings. My recent six-week sojourn in England with its do-it-yourself washing and ironing had left me charitably inclined towards hired help. But this was not the time to say so. "Our home is now too too divine!" exulted Melisande. "It's pragmatic, modern, electrically operated and so easy to manage."

It was certainly different. The beautiful *fin de siècle* period dining table had gone. The replacement gleamed with a laminated top. In a crystal bowl on top were exquisite yellow rose-buds. "No, they are not from the hot-house!" my hostess proclaimed triumphantly. "They are natural plastic. So easy to clean and they give tremendous dimensional stability to my flower arrangements."

"Now for lunch!" she said gaily, switching on an electric mixer. For a few agonizing moments I watched our meal being churned into an indistinguishable pulp before the lid flew open, squirting the floor and me with liberal doses of the concoction. "Occupational hazards!" confessed Melisande, whipping out a garish looking sponge. "Watch this!" she cried, "it's a battery-operated mini vacuum cleaner." It was certainly effective. It mopped up the floor and me, sucking in bits of my attire in the process.

Smoke from the kitchen proclaimed a burnt casserole. Melisande looked crestfallen, and said there was no option but to go out to lunch. Better not risk that mixer again because bits of stainless steel were known to get chipped off the jar and into the food. Besides, if I had to go in for a gastric operation, the National Health Service may not pay for me. So we left the dishes in the sink to enable Algernon to indulge in masses of do-it-yourself joy and went out to eat.

JUDGMENT OF PARIS

The Statesman, November 11, 1977

We would not have chosen the Hotel de la Rome in Paris even in an extravagant dream. But wealthy Parisian friends had booked a room for us. It was evidently their idea of a quiet retreat in a back street. Its plush doors yawned out on the Champs Elysee.

The willowy, coltish receptionist in the marble foyer gazed intensely at us and said the charges were all-inclusive. Service, too. Remember, she breathed, batting her neon-lit eyelashes at my husband, it is not necessary to tip. *Autres temps, autres moeurs*. So far, so good.

A demure little brass birdcage of a lift sedately glided upstairs with us, its prisoners. But once the massive hall porter had stowed our luggage into the room, it was difficult to shrug him away with a casual 'thank you'. We found ourselves paying more than the conventionally prescribed due.

Our room, at first glance, was a dream in sybaritic luxury and refinement, far beyond mundane petit bourgeois thought: ornately carved baroque bedsteads, a Bokharo rug and a profusion of orchids in a vase on a beautiful and seemingly genuine antique writing table. But alas! nightmares soon began to intrude. The call-bell did not ring. The bedside light would not work. In the bathroom, the cistern did not flush and the window remained obstinately shut, hermetically sealing us off from the fresh air of 'gay Paree'. We were to learn that these inflictions were features of the hotel staff's do-it-yourself strategy to bring reluctant tippers to heel. But that knowledge came later.

We complained to the housekeeper. He said he was shocked, amazed and apologetic all at once and he promised instant action.

At lunchtime, a couple of maids appeared to carry out one of the beds. Apparently, an earlier occupant had complained that the springs set off an unholy jingle whenever he turned. But nothing was done to the bell, the light, the cistern and the window. In the course of the day, I was served coffee with liberal blotches of milk, skin floating in the cup while a guest of ours was given lemonade in his whisky. Our dinner, when it arrived, was hot but sans cutlery.

In desperation, my husband suggested tipping the staff, even if we ran out of funds and it meant cutting short our European holiday. They tucked away the generous wad of notes, flashed us dazzling white toothpaste smiles and in no time at all put right all the defects in our room.

Next evening when we returned to the hotel, after having surreptitiously partaken of a frugal meal at a wayside bistro, the chambermaid was deferentially waiting outside our door to usher us in ceremoniously. Obviously ,a rumour had spread that we were of maharajah stock, and consequently needed to be fussed over with many attentions. She wished us good night and then waited hopefully and expectantly. We yielded again.

Next came a knock on the door and in walked the plumber. A short, shifty-eyed creature, he ambled across to the bathroom, whisked open a couple of taps, strolled out leaving shaggy footprints on the floor. Gnashing his dentures, he bid us goodnight. We returned the wishes with a stagey, preoccupied air. He came closer and whimpered that he was a frail old man. We remained unmoved. He said how difficult it was for him to raise his brood of motherless infants. We did not respond.

Next afternoon the cistern collapsed and the tap marked 'froid' let out a torrent of scalding water. My husband now said he could not trust himself to complain because he would probably murder the plumber as well as several of his motherless children. In any case, we could not complain for the bell had again lapsed into silence. The waiter, however, was obligingly waiting in the wings. No sooner had we opened the door than he rushed in. "A thousand pardons!" he cried, gesticulating wildly.

Apparently it was all the plumber's fault. A greater rascal he had never seen, the waiter told us, his voice rising in righteous indignation. "Shame! Shame!" he said, to put us to so much trouble just because he wanted a few extra francs for repairing the cistern. Never mind, he assured us. He would personally arrange for another man to repair it. "Only a question of 15–20 francs" he said.

We knew we had been beaten.

Wealthy Parisien friends had booked us a room in their idea of a quiet hotel. Its plush doors yawned out on the Champs Elysee.

A Visit to Russia brought insight into Soviet Russia as well as its imperial past.

The Nevsky Prospekt in Leningrad (formerly St. Petersburg)

Peter the Great (r. 1682–1725), Czar of all the Russias.

BEAUTIFUL ST. PETERSBURG

The Hindustan Times, September 26, 1982

In Leningrad, we sought accommodation at the Hotel Europa—the gay rendezvous of St. Petersburg nobility in the 1890s. Countless novelists had conjured up its image for us—gorgeous baroque interiors of marble and gold paint ablaze with glittering chandeliers while an orchestra of balalaikas played wildly romantic melodies, while danced exquisitely jewelled ladies and their escorts, officers from the Imperial Chevaliers Gardes, resplendent in white uniforms with silver breast-plates and the Tsarist, double-eagle crested helmets.

Today, the Hotel Europa, silent witness to epoch-making scenes, is a part of the State Intourist Complex. Much of its old exquisite furnishings have gone, swept with the rubble of the past. The floors are stripped of carpeting and the massive mirrors on the walls are visibly brown at the edges. The plush and satin sofas are replaced by a more utilitarian variety. Nevertheless, the saloons remain throbbingly alive, bursting now with tourists from far corners of the world.

Alas for us, the Europa was fully booked and so was the old Hotel Astoria. We were lucky to get a room across the river in the modern Hotel Leningrad. The city was swarming with tourists. They had reason to be. There is little comparable in haunting beauty of this 300 year-old Tsarist capital flung on the Baltic, ten degrees south of the Arctic Circle by Peter the Great. It is a city where dreams and reality meet. The magnificent Italian Renaissance-styled palaces, parks, cathedrals, bridges and boulevards are stately still for all the turns and twists of history. Some of the plush interiors may have been swept away; first by the Revolution and next by Hitler's amputating minions in the Second World War. But the buildings remain, magnificent shells, brooding over memories. The golden spires, domes and cuppolas of another era still soar majestically to the skies. But there were changes too. A doctor can often be found living next door to a tailor. With fine disregard for class differences. A sedate family now lives in the five-room apartment that was once Rasputin's. An air of prim respectability hangs over the place, once the scene of bacchanalian parties. White nylon curtains flutter at the windows and elderly ladies in sombre black trudge up the stairs carrying heavy shopping baskets.

The actual story of St. Petersburg begins in 1703 when Peter the Great, in his search for a modern European capital for his antiquated people had driven up to the shores of the Baltic, to the mouth of the Neva, and declared the site to be worthy of his dreams. It had then presented a desolate scene. The River Neva spread its marshy tentacles far and wide. Neither stone nor labour was easily available for undertaking this ambitious project. Peter, however, was undaunted. He sliced the land by the river with his bayonet and declared, "Here shall be a town." Two hundred thousand labourers died in realising the project. But before 25 years had passed, Peter was ruling from his St. Petersburg.

Towering over the city today, as it did then, is the Fortress of Peter and Paul. Peter himself is buried there along with most other Romanov Tsars. Among exceptions is the ill-fated Nicholas II, the last of them all.

The fortress had dungeons for political prisoners. Among the first was Peter's own son Alexia, suspected of plotting against his father. Peter, who ordered his execution with 40 strokes of the knout, is said to have sobbed at the boy's funeral. More recently in 1887, the jail housed another young lad, Alexander Ulyanov, from a family of hereditary nobles. Alexander was arrested with four other university students in Petersburg for attempting to assassinate Tsar Alexander III. They were caught with a crude bomb hidden inside a hollowed medical text. Alexander was sent to the gallows. Because of his family's aristocratic connections, Alexander could have escaped with a lighter sentence. He, however, insisted on assuming the entire burden of guilt. At the trial he fearlessly declared, "I attempted to kill the Tsar, the attempt failed, that is all there is to it." Alexander's widowed young mother, Maria Ulyanov, herself the daughter of a wealthy landowner, respected her son's decision. She is said to have bravely walked with him to the gallows saying, "Have courage." It was a quality that the Ulyanov family was never found to lack. Maria's second son became known to the world as Vladimir Lenin.

Peter's daughter, Elizabeth, invited the Italian architect Rastrelli to embellish St. Petersburg. The Winter Palace is his most famous creation. It was difficult to imagine that the cobbled Palace Square where the Russian Tsars customarily received their people, now crowded with photo-clicking tourists and their buses, was at the turn of this century the scene of such wanton blood-shedding. It was to this same square that the Socialist priest father Gapon brought his procession of men, women and children on a blistering cold January Sunday in 1905. Carrying banners and icons and singing the anthem "God save the Tsar," they had come hopefully for an audience with their sovereign and saviour, Tsar Nicholas II. Alas! the mounted Cossacks on duty opened fire. Several hundred innocent people were killed and more mutilated. The day came to be known as Bloody Sunday and Russia began the headlong plunge towards revolution.

The Neva embankment is as popular as a strolling ground for young couples today as it was in 1893. How easy it was to imagine twenty-three year-old Lenin, a law apprentice, with his trim beard and his father's frock-coat, walking down this same embankment with an exquisitely fair school-teacher called Krupskaya. Youthful but daring, Krupskaya had first met Lenin at a clandestine Marxist study group meeting at a friend's apartment near Nevsky Prospekt. Like Lenin, Krupskaya also descended from the gentry. Her father had been a military governor of a province in Poland. They were married in exile in Siberia.

Anchored on a quay across the river from our hotel bobbed the demure little naval ship *Aurora,* another landmark of the Revolution. It was the firing of a blank shell on October 24, 1917, that gave a signal to the revolutionaries to take over the Winter Palace, thus ushering in the world's first Communist state.

A TOUCH OF CLASS

The Statesman, April 21, 1979

We finally tracked down the apartment in an old mansion in the heart of Leningrad. The visit was in response to an invitation by our tourist guide. While on the officially-conducted city tour we had hesitantly drawn the lady aside to ask if it was possible for us to visit a typical Russian home. She was plump, middle-aged, cheerful and had seemed reassuringly approachable. Surprisingly, she had answered, "If you like, you can come to mine." It was to prove to be a journey into imperial St. Petersburg.

Nothing had prepared us for this elegant, 19th-century Italian palace with a columned entrance and crested wrought-iron gates. We had gone expecting egalitarian quarters in a tall, concrete apartment house. The place looked a little forlorn now with the paint peeling and the garden ragged with dead leaves choking the marble fountain-place. Nevertheless, it instantaneously evoked for me visions of another era—of a sumptuous blue and gold interior, plush with mahogany and tinkling chandeliers, an ideal setting for an evening of caviar and champagne with an orchestra of balalaikas playing in the background.

A dimly lit foyer opened onto what must once have been the ballroom, for a grand staircase still stood commandingly in the centre. But alas! two concrete walls now marched in parallel lines over the floor, slicing off the hall from either side. The segments seemed to form apartments; for set into the new wall were prim, little wooden doors bearing cardboard nameplates. Twentieth-century's classless realities had asserted themselves.

"How nice you could come!" beamed our hostess drawing us into a cosily cluttered room. A single bulb shed light over a large plastic-covered table, on which the traditional samovar bubbled noisily. "Please do make yourself comfortable. I will get some tea," she said, fussing us into chairs before disappearing into one of the wooden cubicles lining the wall.

It was then that we first became aware of the doll-like old lady lost in a vast armchair by the fireplace. Faded, immobile, she was staring vacantly at the leaping flames. "My mother," explained our guide, who had returned bearing mugs of steaming hot tea. She gave us the mugs, walked over to the old lady, gently prodded her and explained in Russian that we were visitors from India. The old lady slowly raised her head, nodded acknowledgement and went back to her thoughts. "My mother is very old now... over 80," said our guide apologetically. She is little... little, what-do-you-say, forgetful? Absentminded!"

That she was but she had that certain stateliness denied to her daughter. For all the dismally advancing years, she sat upright with a ramrod-like stiffness. High cheek bones stood out prominently beneath the parched skin and the bony, tapering fingers were an alabaster white. She was a ghost but a ghost with an evocative past. I was reminded of one of those lovely pampered heroines from lavish homes which one was constantly reading about in novels on Czarist Russia. The conjecture was not to be far wrong.

Later when talk had veered to our sight-seeing, the old lady had shown a sudden stirring of interest at our mention of a visit to Smolny Institute. "Smolny?" she mused aloud and in perfect French. "How strange... I also once studied there...."

The information no longer came as a surprise. Smolny Institute in the imperial Russia of her youth had been an exclusive finishing-school for young ladies of the Russian nobility. It was turned into Lenin's Bolshevik HQ during the 1917 Revolution.

Smolny Institute for Noble Maidens, a finishing school for the ladies of the aristocracy. These were the last batch of graduates in 1917, after which it became a Bolshevik HQ.

We visit the home of Grigory Rasputin, the Polish peasant-turned priest-turned imperial advisor who played a diabolical role during the last days of Tsarist Russia.

Czar Nicholas II and Czarina Alexandra with their children.

Gregori Rasputin

RASPUTIN REMEMBERED

The Times of India, October 21, 1979

SIXTY-FOUR DZERZHINSKY STREET turned out to be a massive, five-storeyed apartment house in the heart of Leningrad. An imposing columned door marked the entrance. Poised directly above was a three-tier cluster of half-moon balconies. The windows had the cornices typical of Italian Renaissance mansions of 19th-century St. Petersburg. There was little, however, to proclaim the building as the home of an extraordinary imperial favourite: the priest Rasputin.

What a strange contrast these surroundings presented, I thought, to the flamboyant legend that was Rasputin, and the glittering tsarist palaces he was known to frequent! Yet it was from a five-roomed apartment in this building that Rasputin controlled the destinies of Russia in those fateful years before the October Revolution of 1917 which was to change the face of the modern world.

In his lifetime Rasputin had earned many names: a "startzy" or a man of God, a demon of the flesh, a saint with miraculous powers, a double-faced Janus, debauchee and a Machiavellian king-maker. One fact does emerge clearly—between 1914–16, Rasputin was all powerful in imperial Russia. Grand dukes, senior army generals, bishops, princes, prima-donnas and politicians cringed before him. To incur Rasputin's displeasure was to court dismissal. Tales of his bacchanalian orgies and his political manipulations gathered momentum. But no outrage by the public nor entreaties by the Tsar's closest relatives seemed to be able to discredit him. To their imperial majesties Nicholas II and Alexandria, Rasputin was the Holy Man.

Secure in this knowledge, Rasputin strutted through marble and mahogany palaces of the nobility. An earthy, coarse, pock-marked Siberian peasant with long unkempt hair and dressed in gaudily coloured silk blouses, he cut a strikingly different figure in this gilded world. Around his neck was a heavy gold chain with a gold cross, a present from the Tsarina herself. A ripe unwashed smell oozed from his body. His eyes were his most compelling feature: they hypnotised, caressed, threatened, lured, elevated and terrified. Nobody could remain indifferent to him.

"Dzerzhinsky street?" asked the surprised Russian taxi driver. He had never heard of any tourists wanting to go there. Neither had he heard of Rasputin. He belonged to modern Russia—young, vibrant and impatient of tradition.

Our nippy little Zhugali sped us across the elegant Trinity Bridge towards the south embankment. Below us the mighty River Neva glinted in the September sun. In Rasputin's days, I had read that fur-clad couples of the tsarist nobility bundled into brightly-coloured troikas to speed over the frozen river to attend a party at one of the many sumptuous, chandelier-lit city palaces. The palaces are still all there; only now they have been divided into apartments for the proletariat.

It may have been an evening of baccarat, of dancing to an orchestra of balalaikas, but nobody left till the early hours of the morning. Then it was bed until noon, when the day began with a clandestine canter in the park. Then another round of pleasure in the evening. Perhaps a ballet at the Marinsky theatre. Rasputin was often the heart and soul of the party.

We passed the elegant pale-green and gold, 900-roomed Winter Palace, once the official residence of the Tsar of All the Russias. Now it is the Hermitage Museum. No. 64 Dzerzhinsky was only three blocks away and consisted of two buildings, one directly behind the other. It was on the third floor of the smaller one at the back that Rasputin lived. Today a cemented courtyard links the two buildings. Once frequented by the aristocracy, the paved courtyard is now a children's cycling ground. Three TV antennas sprouted from the roof-top of Rasputin's apartment, and from an open window fluttered scalloped nylon curtains. A smell of borsch and meat solianka wafted down from under a closed door. The general air was one of prim respectability.

Felix Yussupov, the fabulously wealthy prince who married the Tsar's niece and who was to murder Rasputin on a cold winter night in 1916, was a frequent visitor to Rasputin's home. In a book, Felix describes the apartment as being small and surprisingly sedate, furnished with narrow wooden beds, painted chests and crudely-made icons. He writes that "it had an air of middle-class solidity". Rasputin lived there with his daughter Marie, who after the Revolution, escaped to America and became a famous lion-tamer.

Like all members of the royal family, Felix had watched with alarm Rasputin's increasing control over the empress, and through her, the emperor and the entire machinery of statecraft. Rasputin's reckless top-level political appointments and dismissals were tilting the country headlong towards anarchy. In the closing weeks of

The sumptous Winter Palace on the Neva in St. Petersburg, which houses the Hermitage Museum today.

Czar Nicholas II and Czarina Alexandra dressed for their last great ball at the Winter Palace in 1903.

The horrific Bloody Sunday Massacre in January 1905. A peaceful march to the palace led by a priest Father Gapon was mercilessly gunned down by the Imperial guard.

Posters of the Czar and Czarina in the clutches of Rasputin began appearing in St. Petersburg.

The outbreak of the Revolution of 1917 led by soldiers and peasants.

December 1916, the young prince arranged to kill Rasputin in an underground cellar in his palace in Petersburg. When poisoned cakes and wine failed to do the trick, an attempt was made to shoot him. Still the victim writhed with life. The terrified murderers tied the body, dug a hole in the frozen river and pushed the ghastly bundle in. The medical verdict was that Rasputin had died of drowning!

The rise of Grigori Rasputin from an obscure moujik of Pokrovskoie to becoming the Chief Imperial Advisor is bizarre: only the extraordinary combination of circumstances prevailing in the last decade of imperial Russia offer some clue. The gentle but ineffective Tsar Nicholas II and his strong-willed, unpopular, German-born empress ruled over a jaded aristocracy juxtaposed with a brooding, sullen and hungry countryside, with dark pent-up forces waiting like coiled springs to unleash themselves. Rasputin first appeared in St. Petersburg in 1904. The perfumed and pomaded aristocracy, bored by their hectic round of balls, baccarat, theatre and gossip found in him an exciting diversion. He was certainly an unusual man of God.

The word 'Rasputin' in Russian means dissolute, a fact he used to his advantage. He had sinned and repented and therefore was better equipped to lead frail mortals to God. Father John of Kronstadt, the highly respected father confessor to Tsar Alexander III was among the first to welcome Rasputin.

Rasputin first met their Imperial Majesties in November 1906. In August that year, the empress had given birth at last after four daughters to a male heir and thereby crowned a 10 year-marriage. At first Rasputin made scant impact upon their Imperial Majesties. However, the young Tsarvich's near-fatal haemorrhage while the royal family was holidaying in a hunting lodge in the Polish woods in 1912 changed all this. The child made an inexplicable and miraculous recovery. The empress came away convinced that it was all due to the power of Rasputin's prayers. After that there was no turning back for Rasputin.

Today the tradition of 'Startzy', the man of God, has been swept away into history. St. Petersburg's famous cathedral of Our Lady of Kazan is now the Museum of the History of Religion and Atheism. So is the St. Issac's Cathedral built as a replica of St. Peter's at Rome. Instead of the traditional mass-chanting, candle-holding congregation, photo-clicking tourists like us tread through its magnificent interiors. Gone are the gold-robed bishops with gem-encrusted crosses and priests with long beards trailing incense pots. But golden icons and frescoes continue to adorn the walls, radiating a fiery, blazing glow.

There are places of worship in Leningrad, our tourist guide assured us. The city has a practising Roman Catholic church, a Baptist church, a Jewish synagogue, a mosque and even a Buddhist temple! Orthodox Russian ritual, we were told, survives in the onion-domed Trinity Cathedral which was said to be Rasputin's favourite. Also known as the 'Church of the Spilled Blood,' the Trinity was built in memory of the Tsar-liberator, Alexander II, who was killed on that spot by a nihilist bomb in 1881. Rasputin also met his fate near here at Prince Felix's palace, just a stone's-throw away.

AMERICAN LIFE

An undertaker in upstate New York tantalized us with tempting "offers". An ebony casket, specially recorded "Hare Rama" chants and sandlewood incense sticks during the last rites and a procession of gleaming chauffeur-driven black limousines for the final journey.

PAY NOW, DIE LATER

The Illustrated Weekly of India, June 26, 1975

We were in New York State driving down a typical American main street compounded by rows of service stations, parking lots, used car lots, a cafe with a cutout cowboy on top, a restaurant inside a giant wigwam and vast shopping plazas. Then we came across a gracious white country mansion with a large rotating sign on top. It sternly asked: "Have you reserved your grave?"

Intrigued and agog we stopped by. In the elaborate oak-panelled hall, piped music relayed sombre strains from Verdi's *Requiem*.

The proprietor, a tall stout man with a great mop of curly hair and a huge bristling moustache, came bounding across the room to us. "Your servant," he said with a bow. "Burt's the name." He wore a porkpie hat and a carnation in his buttonhole. Otherwise he had none of those morbid protractions generally associated with an undertaker. On the contrary, he was full of *joie de vivre*, very disturbingly like a door-to-door salesman.

"Looking for a place in the Heavenly Home?" he asked with disconcerting cheer.

"Uh, huh," said my husband guardedly.

A Very Permanent Purchase

"Very wise, very wise," nodded our friend. "After all, this is a very permanent purchase. It's never too early to start planning, not that you look as though you'll require it for quite some time to come. But then you never can tell. Why, only the other day, we had this young man browsing in our Coffins Section, lovingly fingering a casket with a quilted satin interior. "How about signing up on our new Economy Package Deal?" I say to him. 'Not now,' he says. 'I'll come again next week.' He sure does. But alas, as a corpse!"

He explained the vagaries of human life to us in soothing, professionally impersonal gestures. Our health, he said, looked good. Age was on our side. He did not mean to frighten us. But heart attacks were becoming a common occurrence. And cancer....

Burt picked up a printed form and began his inquisition. "What are you thinking of? Interment or Incineration?"

"The latter," replied my husband recklessly.

"Ah, you must be a Hindu!" he exclaimed triumphantly. "I have just the thing for you. We can arrange to have the 'Hare Krishna Hare Rama' chant played during the last rites. Shall I also make a note that incense be lighted? We offer sandalwood, jasmine and rose. With Burt there, you'll have nothing to worry. All we ask is to be informed as soon as the client is dead.

"Now one word about the plots. We can offer a decent one in our special park for $500 a piece. It's cheaper, however, to take the double one. We always advise our married couples to do that. Provisions can also be made for children and favourite pets. Why, only the other day, we had to make arrangements to accommodate a horse with its owner!

"We even have a new installment Payment Plan which might interest you," he suggested.

"You mean pay now and die later?"

Burt handed us a couple of brochures outlining the services offered. The First Class client qualified for an ebony casket, fresh flowers, three days' repose in a luxurious carpeted air-conditioned parlour with period chairs for callers, prayer books, live organ music and a procession of chauffeur-driven black limousines for the final procession to the 'Heavenly Home'. The service also included insertion of notices in newspapers, fees for the clergyman and engraved Thank You cards of acknowledgement to be sent out by the bereaved family.

Embalmment is a part of the fare and Burt throws in a special extra: pedicure, manicure, hair-styling and make-up "free of charge". Surely another $250 is not too much for the special services of a Master Cosmetician in "fixing facial expression to order". This service applies only to the Golden deluxe customers.

If the client opts for the Economy Class, however, he has to let nature take its own course and hope for the best. Apart from freezing the face into a perpetual smile, the Economy Class offers its client most of the "regular" services: air-conditioned comfort, prayer books, music, but there is no mention of "perpetual care of the graves" as a part of the purchase price. The Economy client, while entitled to free notices in newspapers, gets "no break on the digging charges". Flowers are provided. But they are waxed.

If a client wants a gold-plated casket, he must subscribe to Burt's "Golden deluxe"; that is, if he does not mind spending a lifetime's savings on "Eternal Sleep". There are other things upon which a millionaire can dissipate his money. If his fancy veers to exotic orchids flown in from Tahiti, he can obtain these as well.

Burt suddenly came bounding out of his little office like a cuckoo from a clock: "Now for the locales. I've got some real super ones to show you." He shepherded us into his black limousine which looked suspiciously like a funeral car and drove us off to a tranquil park.

Tenderness Hill

Welcome to Tenderness Hill, said our inexhaustible host. "How would you like that quiet secluded spot beneath the elms?"

Always the pragmatic salesman, he continued: "To give local colour, we have even provided a village chapel. We had it imported all the way from England: the stones, the timber, the bell, the lot. There's nothing we wouldn't do for a client! Of course, the closer you get to the chapel, the more expensive your plot gets."

Burt's voice took on a sonorous, seductive tone: "Can you imagine yourself lying in deep slumber, dreaming of gurgling brooks and thatched cottages, drinking deeply at the well of calm sweetness? Kinda Wordsworthian, eh?"

He suddenly came down to earth, "Our monument-maker can provide you with a marble footstone which will carry your name. If you like our Antique Touch, he will do the lettering in olde English and smudge it to make it look real old."

Our lack of enthusiasm disconcerted Burt. "Ah, perhaps you would like brightlights, the noise, the bustle. I keep forgeting that you are both so young!

"Not to worry, I have a place for you. Right near the Highway. You can say hullo to the folks as they whiz by. Besides, next to you is a jolly old friend of mine. Full of jokes and funny stories he was. He'll simply kill you with his laughter."

Sketches by Mario Miranda.

By now, we were reduced to total silence. He looked perturbed. After all, we could be some dispossessed royalty with a convenient bank balance tucked away in Switzerland.

"We even go in for mausoleums and that kind of thing, you know! Not your Taj Mahals, of course. But we don't do too badly either. Last year we had this meat-packing millionaire from Chicago who wanted a real swank palace. He even had his carpets and art treasures moved in. The joint had to be made earthquake and fire-proof. And do you know what?" he asked dropping into a furtive whisper, "we ever fitted in a hi-fi system to carry an echo—for atmosphere. Kinda spooky, I thought, but a customer is a customer."

Cold Storage Facilities

He suddenly looked apologetic and confessed: "I haven't got any cold storage facilities."

"Cold storage?" I asked incredulously.

"Yes, for preservation. Ever since some semi-wise guy wrote that piece in *The Reader's Digest*, folks are getting hot and bothered all the time. Only yesterday we got this phone call from a dame wanting us to preserve her and her poodle so that they can be resurrected together. Fancy that!"

For a minute Burt sounded old and defeated. But recovered soon.

"We at Burt's will also be in a position to offer all these facilities. Just you wait for a year. My son is finishing his diploma in Funeral Management before joining the family business."

I remembered *The Sleeping Beauty* and wondered if Burt's services could also provide a Prince Charming to bring the dead princess back to life one day....

THE CAPTIVE HUSBAND

The Illustrated Weekly of India, September 19, 1976

"WANTED: A HOUSE-SPOUSE for a successful young lady executive," said the ad in the matrimonial column of a newspaper we picked up at the Grand Central Station in New York. We were on our way upstate to New Jersey to look up old friends we had not met for ten years. "Full financial security guaranteed, provided the male partner is a good cook and will not expect help with the dish-washing. He must be agreeable to moving house if wife takes a job in another town, get up if the baby cries at night (if and when the need be) and help the kids with their homework at least three nights a week. Age no bar. Widowers acceptable so long as they have no dogs and/or children." The advertiser ends with an enticing bait to the suitable candidate—a promise of a colour TV for the kitchen.

I feel as though we are in some topsy-turvy world. The illusion persists when we arrive at our destination and our friend Bill opens the door. He has a frilly apron round his waist, bread-crumbs in his hair and the harassed expression of a suburban housewife disturbed in the act of shovelling food into the mouth of a squealing infant. But his face brightens up on seeing us. "Hullo! Hullo!" he cries in an excited little voice, "but how wonderful to see you folks again! Laura should be back any minute. Come right in, dearies." He opens the door wide.

"Uh, huh," says my husband guardedly.

Victoriana

Bill leads us into a heavily draped room. The decor is somewhat baroque, with an accent on pink-satin tapestried chairs, marble urns and cupids and couches piled high with tasselled cushions. Pictures are everywhere, covering the piano and standing three deep on an occasional table: pictures of two cherubic babies, a group picture of the boys grown up and at school, a somewhat faded wedding picture of Laura and Bill.

We are taken aback at the change. In this gentle self-effacing creature, with his concave chest and adenoidal voice, we find it difficult to trace the Bill of the picture—the Bill we knew 12 years ago, that dashing Johnny Weissmuller with an ecstatic bride clinging adoringly to his arm. But alas! that was before the clarion call of Women's Lib and Reverse Roles was heard across the land.

Unaware of the trend of our thoughts, Bill asks wistfully: "Hope you 1ike my parlour?"

"Well," says my husband cautiously, looking at the pink Victoriana, "you could say it is a... a period piece."

Bill continues: "Laura prefers more mod stuff. Things like tribal wall-hangings, abstract murals, and low divans covered with scratchy rough fabrics, you know. But she is not one to dictate. Oh no, not Laura. Why, she says, 'Bill, you are the master in the house, so you must decide.' Not like one of those wives forever interfering."

"Laura should be back any minute now," repeats Bill, fussing us into comfortable chairs by the fire. "She gets a bit delayed now and then. After all, she's something real big in the city now!" A possessive pride creeps into his voice.

He brings out a tin of cakes with the coffee. They are delicious and we say so. Bill smiles deprecatingly: "Of course, with all those instant mixes so readily available in the supermarket cooking is not so difficult. I, of course, prefer to make my own at home. It is so much more wholesome."

He then settles down in his rocking-chair, pulls out his knitting, fixes his glasses midway on the bridge of his nose and volunteers with a dash of wistful nostalgia: "Gcc! Things havc surc changed since you were last here. Womenfolk are really going after us men in a big way. Short of throwing rolling-pins at us, they stop at nothing!" Bill laughs. "There are unions and strikes and what-have-you all over the place. The latest in our town is the formation of the 'Federation of Husbands of the World Unite' to combat the tyranny of the 'Feminist League' whose battle-cry is 'Revolution against Male Chauvinism—Must Begin in the Home!' Holy cow! You should attend one of their sessions. It's kinda real fierce!"

"And do you know the latest?" Bill draws forward his chair, his voice dropping to a furtive whisper. "Young couples have started drawing up contracts with their lawyers before marriage to outlinc each other's duties! Things like who should do the weekly vacuuming, how many evenings should each parent devote to baby-sitting, who will pick up the groceries and who will dump the garbage. Really! What is the world coming to?" Bill rolls his eyes. "We have even heard of a wife threatening to go to court just because her husband mulishly refused to teach their child the

Sketches by Mario Miranda.

Humpty-Dumpty nursery rhymes on the day it was his turn to help with the kid's homework! Now, tell me," says Bill sanctimoniously, "how long can the first flush of newly wedded love survive such protracted legal negotiations?" Bill had a point.

When Laura got an offer for this fabulous job upstate, Bill willingly gave up his own to help house and look after the kids. Things had worked out rather well for them, Bill confided primly. Laura was a good provider and always made it a point to come home before it was time for the kids to go to bed. Now that the boys were away in school, she often gave a hand with the dishes, even though the poor dear had such a busy day at the office. "You must give it a try some time," Bill advises helpfully. My husband mutters darkly something which sounds suspiciously like East is East and West is West and never the twain can meet.

The bell rings and Laura sweeps in, enveloping us in her friendly charm. "Too-too divine having you again," she flutes, flinging herself on me with a bear-like hug. She wears large horn-rimmed glasses, the characteristic insignia of all successful commercial executives, and a brisk businesslike bun on the nape of her slender neck.

Bill obediently plods across to the kitchen to get coffee. "I hope he's been looking after you," Laura asks solicitously. Of course, of course, we say hastily. Bill was a jewel, says Laura. She really does not know how she could cope without him. "I can't tell you what a paragon he is around the house a real walking gadget! Whether it is fixing a leaking tap or whipping up a soufflé, there's no one like Bill." Laura smiles proudly.

I look speculatively at my husband. The last time he had been called upon to mend an electric fuse, he had successfully plunged our entire neighbourhood in total darkness. I now wonder if it was his own do-it-yourself insurance against being called to help with domestic chores.

"Bill is so thoughtful, so considerate," continues Laura. "Spoiling me, laying out my bath-salts, picking up my favourite authors from the local library and even serving breakfast in bed!"

Bill blushes a bright peony at the praise. "Shucks, honey. It's nothin'."

Evening shadows lengthen and Bill bustles off to fix dinner. After an initial "Oh, please don't bother" in the breathless voice of a little girl, Bill succumbs to our offer of help. Laura too joins us. She has peeled off her glasses and the peroxide-blonde wig. With her naturally curly brown hair tumbling down in a dusky halo around her little face and those enormous blue forget-me-not eyes twinkling puckishly, she seems once again the Laura we knew. She had been a dewy-eyed bride then with fully developed fantasies about being an ultra-feminine ornament of her little castle; her Bill, the king and the bread-winner, the you-Tarzan-me-Jane relationship.

The curtains, drawn up against the night, sealed off the outside world. A conspiratorial air seems to invade the darkly carpeted and candle-lit dining room. We feel like subversive plotters against a revolution. The good food and fire were having their effect in transporting us back in time and space. Laura, momentarily forgetting her allegiance to her Revolutionary Sisters, talks with apologetic nostalgia of those days when she could safely see her man off at nine o'clock in the morning before settling down to a cosy little chat with the nice Mrs. Smith from next door. And Bill ruminates about the times when the way to his lady-love's heart was through the muscle-building chest-expander.

The bell rings again. "That must be Alexandra," cries Laura, jumping to her feet. "Alexandra is one of the Revolutionary Sisters, actually she is the Mentor. When she heard you were coming, she said she was very keen to meet you."

I look distinctly alarmed. I belong to that clan of unemancipated, non-career women who do not mind doing the marketing, darning socks and taking kids to the dentist so long as my husband continues to protect, cherish and bring in the monthly pay-packet.

But Alexandra is already upon us. As a protest against the brazen exploitation of 'femininity', she wears a shapeless tunic of coarse wool. Her lips are thickened by white salve. A highly successful and glamorous chairperson of an advertising agency by day, Alexandra carried the banner of Women's Lib into uninitiated homes by night.

Accompanying her is her male secretary, a slender, dark young man called Alain. He exudes clouds of patchouli. "Alain, come and meet everybody," cooes Alexandra. Alain waves one manicured hand at the company. With the other he is busy lighting a cigarette in a holder. He then glides across the room and envelops us in a blue stare. Can I feel my husband shudder! As for Bill, he has retreated within his concave frame. "So you are from India?" says Alexandra. Her tone is portentous with meaning. "Why don't we go to your study, Laura, and have a nice chat."

"Yes, yes," says Laura in considerable dismay. "Just as you like, Alexandra."

Because of our guest's growing autocracy and my curiosity, I obediently follow, leaving the men folk with the after-dinner dish-washing.

"Come with us, Alain dear," commands Alexandra. "The poor boy needs every little respite he can get from our fearfully busy schedule," she offers by way of explanation. Alain follows with alacrity, waving a ringed hand at our startled spouses.

Heretic

Alexandra quickly gets down to business. She explains the Movement with illustrative gestures. "Now take yourself," she smiles encouragingly. "You have had a college education and a degree from abroad. But you've got married and acquired a family before you've had time to settle down to a career and assert your identity. You have allowed yourself to become 'A Captive Wife'." Alexandra fixes me with a severe eye.

I do not have the courage to protest that I enjoy my role.

"You must assert yourself," says Alexandra. "You must not allow yourself to become a victim of our male-dominated society.

"Why should women be the ministering angels of the household?" she sternly asks. "The tender, loving and sensitive partners? Why should God be addressed as Him? Why shouldn't History be renamed Herstory? Why should female models be used in TV ads for detergents? We must Protest, Revolt, Fight for our Rights."

Some time later we heard that Alexandra had run away with a macho swimming instructor and now spent her days relaxing by the pool gazing in rapt adoration as he coaxed nubile young maidens to practise their breast stroke.

IF ONLY LOOKS COULD KILL

The Statesman, October 5, 1976

A CHARITY RAFFLE TICKET once won me a free visit to a beauty parlour. The gift card promised a Top-to-Toe treatment which would enable the recipient to leap into the rarefied heights of the beautiful. Rather like Cinderella's magic transformation. Untried by calamity and excited with fantasies, I turned up at the appointed place, a discreet pink salon resplendent with a sign that proclaimed, "By appointment to filmstar R...." The chief beautician stylishly called M'zelle, eyed me with the grave discretion of an undertaker. I, on my part, seeing her emaciated face, began to have serious misgivings about her virtues as an arbiter of beauty. But it was too late.

M'zelle explained my face to me with soothing, professionally impersonal, illustrative gestures. The eyes, basically, she said, were not bad. However, a little eye-shadow perhaps...? The brows could certainly do with a little shaping. She smiled encouragingly. My hair, of course, left much to be desired. But the nose! She gazed heavenwards in genuine despair. Had I never heard of plastic surgery? A shapely new nose could easily replace the old one.

"Now let's get on with the job," she announced cheerfully. "Before we've finished with you, I am hoping we will be able to dispel that drab housewifely look!" The fears deepened. I was handed into the arms of a massive Madonna masseuse from distant Hanover. This good matron enjoyed a reputation for being able to tone up the limbs of her clients so vigorously that they quaked like a jellied confection. And, by jove, she did it too.

I was now declared fit for the next stage—the Turkish Bath. This torture chamber with its relentless agonies brought to life my vision of Dante's Purgatory. I was, however, not alone in my penance; stretched along the length of the narrow room were several hunks of flesh broiling away. I was allotted a bench and given the dubious pleasure of watching the slow dissolution of my plump well-nurtured body.

The steaming done, the victim is smothered in towelling and escorted to M'zelle herself for the last rites. Then it was a question of sitting agonizingly still while M'zelle wielded her implements over the facial topography. She was gregariously chatty that morning. Deftly stroking a fine brush over my eyes, she threw out the useful information that her salon was equipped to cater for weddings with a 'Special Package Bridal Make-up'. Had I a friend who was planning to get married? If so, M'zelle could dress the bride, beautify her plainer unmarried sisters, smarten up her mother and even make a young man of her father by dyeing his hair. What could be more fetching, she sternly asked, than a handsome bridal party? Think of all the marriage offers that the family's spinsters, gathering dust on a shelf for so long but now suddenly preening in painted glory, would be able to command? M'zelle had a point. Though I must confess that my heart went out to the poor innocent groom and his sense of cold shock when he first set eyes upon his bride minus eyebrows, eyelashes and perhaps also, her crowning glory.

There was little time, however, to indulge in these speculations. M'zelle threw down her tools and dramatically exclaimed, "Ah now! Look at you! The new, beautiful you!"

I looked at myself. The mirror was not reassuring. My dry and lanky hair had been puffed out into a disturbingly large Bardot beehive. My face with its bushy brows now thinly arched and its smudged eyes was painted beyond recognition. But because of Mzelle's growing autocracy and my collapsing resistance. I did not protest.

Nor did my story have the conventional Cinderella ending. Alas! My spouse did not gaze upon the transformation with the rapt adoration that had been promised. Instead, he exclaimed with the familiarity born of 12 years of matrimony, "Goodness! what on earth have you gone and done to yourself?"

EVERLASTINGLY WRONGED

The Times of India, September 21, 1963

In a sudden spurt of nostalgia. I went to visit my old school and my schoolteacher Mrs. Cinnathambi. The good lady said, "Well, well, you are quite a grown-up girl now! Let me see, you have done your B.A.? M.A.? Excellent! Excellent! No doubt you will want to teach now. What? Don't like to teach? What nonsense is that? Why, when I was your age I was burning, simply burning with a desire to teach. Well! Well! What you really need is a chance, just one chance to teach and you can take my word for it my girl, you will want to teach all your life. I go away on a teachers' conference from tomorrow so you can begin by taking over my fifth formers."

"But, Mrs. Cinnathambi...."

"They are a lovable and an intelligent lot, passionately interested in Things Inspiring, Things of the Spirit... you know, like poetry, painting...."

"But, Mrs. Cinnathambi...."

"All you have to do is to take their poetry lesson, make them write a couple of essays in class, goad them to be more creative and, of course, discourage Mohan's mother from calling on you too often. Tactfully, mind you; Mohan's father is one of the trustees of the school."

The next morning in class, before I could begin my thought-provoking discussion on the nature of poetry, one boy, whose name I later learnt was Mohan, stood up and said, "Don't you think all this business about appreciating poetry is a regular racket?" The whole class then quietly waited for my views. I cleared my throat and began, "Poetry is the sublimest of arts. There is nothing more elevating than a beautiful poem...." Mohan politely interrupted me with, "Miss, after all, do you have to be so formal with us? Mrs. Cinnathambi is away, you know."

In the afternoon I gave my pupils an essay to write on a game of cricket they had seen. Twenty-seven out of twenty-eight half-hearted descriptions of games of cricket that I received embodied the injured air of race everlastingly wronged. Why on earth did teachers persist in their belief that young people still liked cricket? When would we realise that the game had become frightfully old fashioned now? But then, living as we did in such a narrow little realm of books, it was perhaps too much to expect us to know the ways of the world at large. The twenty-eighth essay was original, to say the least. It said, "Rain all day. No game."

I tried to explain, "When I asked you to write this essay I did not except you to be literally true."

The next afternoon during the lunch recess Mohan's mother came to see me. "So, you are the new teacher? You are an M.A.? Good. Studied modern literature for your degree, didn't you? Ah… I did wonder where all those new ideas came from. But tell me, you did go to school here?"

"Yes, I did."

"Then don't you remember being taught to believe it is a sin to tell a lie?" she asked severely.

"But, of course."

"Then, why, did you ask my little boy to write untruths in his exercise yesterday?"

"That's ridiculous," I protested. "I never…."

She learned forward, lowered her voice and went on darkly, "Would you like my son to be punished in hell?"

Trying another approach, I said with an attempt at humour, "Wouldn't do the young man much harm, would it?"

There was an ominous silence in the room. A few minutes later Mohan's mother recovered herself and quietly went away. I was left alone to recollect uneasy emotions in tranquillity.

ENFANTS TERRIBLES

The Times of India, May 2, 1964

Of all the experiments with baths the most hair-raising is trying to bathe one's little nephews and nieces, What? A bath? Once again? exclaim the little cherubs, and, judging from their expressions, there seems to be no greater torture imaginable on earth. But if you must insist, they continue with gentle resignation, could not they have it all together in the big bathtub in Grandpa's bathroom?

Grandma's Kindness

Before a disciplinarian foot can be put down on such rash ventures, Grandma hears the plea and grants the request at once. For the grown-up sent to supervise, the proceedings call for two hands, two feet and six senses.

The children generally begin by throwing water on the clothes laid out for them to wear after the bath, on the on the bathroom floor, and on you. They fight over the soap, send it slithering down the wet floor, race after it, fall one on top of the other, and graze Bharat's knee. Bharat lets out a heart-rending cry and has to be coaxed back to a better frame of mind with a chocolate. The others feel the occasion calls for an all-round distribution. The chocolates are eaten, the wrappers thrown into the bathtub, and the sticky fingers wiped on the walls.

Gouri then picks up the forgotten soap, drops it into the tub and looks surprised. The others immediately dive into the water as though their whole lives depend on getting to the soap. Of course, they have to be fished out for they still have all their clothes on.

By this time, the water in the tub is so messy that it has to be changed. Vikram obligingly turns on the tap but forgets to remove the plug. The havoc-makers then sit on the floor, giggle and nearly strangle themselves trying to strip off their wet clothes. Meanwhile, water overflows from the tub, spills down on the bathroom floor and make its merry way towards the bedroom.

The Wrong Boat

When finally the tap has been turned off, the water mopped and the little ones dropped into the tub, it occurs to Bharat that he would like to have his sailing boat. You find a boat and hand it to him and he cries it is the wrong boat. What he wants is his new red boat. You look for the new red boat. By this time, Radhika has waddled out of the bathroom and made her wet and destructive way across the new carpet. She wants *her* boat. She takes Vikram along too. Gouri begins to cry then because no one has remembered to bring hers.

Bharat calls her a crybaby, and Gouri smacks him. A fierce and lively warfare commences. The others join in determined not to miss any of the fun. Sponges are hurled into the air, soap cakes fly past. The sound and the fury of it would put any border warfare to shame. Several grown-ups arrive on the spot to take stock of the situation. After much effort, the contenders are separated, scrubbed, washed, dried and clothed.

The Angels

Half an hour later they creep upstairs to the puja room where Grandma sits in prayer, blissfully unaware of the pandemonium that has raged below. They silently kneel on the floor; hands folded in prayer, heads bowed. Judging by their expression they look like angels come down upon earth. Grandma cannot resist the sight. She opens out her arms to them and they go and nestle against her, their faces reflecting a profound harmony with one another and the world in general.

Grandma pops *prasad* into their mouths, hugs them warmly and says it's a wicked shame that people in our house complain the way they do about the children.

A DO-IT-YOURSELF SOUVENIR

The Statesman, October 12, 1968

One evening, we discovered that a clock was stolen from our flat. Our neighbours made a fearful fuss and insisted we call in the police rightaway. Because of their touching faith and growing insistence my husband and I made our way to the police station. A constable approached the counter with schooled deliberation, moved a register from one side to another, glanced at his watch, and said, "Yes?"

He listened to us with tired patience and said he was sorry he merely did the night beat and could do nothing about thieves breaking into people's homes during the day. It was simply not in his department.

Crouched at the back and poring over masses of papers was a prematurely greying policeman. He looked as though he would enjoy nothing more than an afternoon at the movies, watching Waheeda Rehman frolic with Dharmendra over verdant pastures of Aarey Milk Colony, far away from swarthy black-bearded murderers whose photographs it was his lot to paste in albums all day.

"Don't ask me," he immediately protested to us in a long-suffering voice of one conscious of doing his duty while others fiddled. His job was simply to file papers and case-histories of notorious bandits and he had no idea of clock thieves.

Finally, we were directed to the Sherlock Holmes of the station, who pulled out a foul-smelling pipe in keeping with convention and proceeded to listen to our tale of woe. His eyes were glued to a criminal photographic record lying open upon his desk. From time to time be would glance at us in a speculative way and trigger off a rapid question, all most unerving.

"What has gone?" he asked for the sixth time.

"A... a watch," I nervously began.

"A watch?" he asked, alert and suspicious all at once, as if he always suspected something fishy about us. "No, no a clock," I hastily amended.

Eventually, Sherlock Holmes was convinced of our legitimacy to the claim. He handed us a long and elaborate form to be filled out in triplicate, requiring information about our private income, the number of dependents, the birthplace of a paternal ancestor and the varieties of clocks purchased by the family since World War II. No sooner was it completed than he seized it from our hands, stamped it and handed us back two copies, his face now a bored inscrutable mask of the stereotype bureaucrat. His stern adieu was, "Do not call us. We will call you."

When three whole months had passed without their calling us we wrote back a gentle reminder. After another three months came the reply:

Dear Sir,

We are in receipt of your letter of March 27, 1967. We beg to inform you that your communication has been sent to the Central Bureau of Investigation and is scheduled for reading on July 25, 1967.

Subsequent study of the case will also be undertaken by the Central Finger Print Bureau.

In future, when corresponding kindly indicate your complaint registration number, age, occupation and permanent and temporary addresses.

We brought out the copies of forms we had filled at the station and carefully put them away in a box marked personal treasures: they were our own do-it-yourself souvenirs from the police.

The new rich are obsessed with the wish to buy a way of life very different from the one to which they were born. Money comes quick; culture takes at least two generations.

VOL. XCI 44 SUNDAY, NOVEMBER 1, 1970 ESTD. 1880 PRICE 85 PAISE

The Illustrated Weekly of India

The Newly Rich

THE DESIRE TO BELONG

The Illustrated Weekly of India,
November 1, 1970

One of the marked changes among the nouveau riche of today is a driving concern for better living. Prosperous merchants, who at one time were content to eke out an austere and joint family living in a tiny hovel overlooking a malodorous street, now own a chain of luxury apartments in the city's elite quarter.

Dhoti-clad businessmen, who sprawled on gaddis stroking their hairy bellies as they played a leisurely game of flush on Sunday afternoons, now bravely squeeze themselves into raw silk sherwanis in order to be seen at the opening of the French film festival. Women, who lived in perpetual hibernation in the kitchen bemoaning the woe that was mother-in-law, now wear backless cholis exposing an indecent lot of flesh and accompany their husbands to parties where they sit silently on one side of the room, while the men congregate on the other side.

Independent India has thrown up a vast army of new business entrepreneurs—a class of tough, greedy, semi-educated, hustling men, inexhaustibly ambitious and immensely successful in spinning quick money. Having made a pile, they no longer seem to want it all safely tucked away in various banks, joint stock companies, under mattresses and under the bathroom tiles. Now they wish to wrest a place for themselves in a society once monopolised by the elite I.C.S. men, zamindars, brown sahebs and maharajas.

A few years ago the disparity between the patrician and the trader was precisely marked and universally accepted. The only passport upward, if at all, lay in owning land and that too for several generations. But not so now.

All The Trappings

With new ideas, new energy, new money the nouveau riche are bursting into the citadels of the landed gentry, and buying up their paintings and their palaces. A great deal that is brash and hybrid, consequently, stems from their exercises in quick social climbing; a disturbing obsession being to collect a vast assortment of bric-a-brac whose possession for some inexplicable reason, is felt to truly legalise one's position in society.

Restaurant owners welcome them as they order food indiscriminately, specially those dishes cunningly disguised under stupefying French names. "They come and buy everything that is new and gimmicky," says a boutique proprietor, "the shinier and bigger a thing, the better it must be: seems to be their purchasing motto. But they are never too proud to accept advice or to learn."

But not all nouveau riche are upstarts. Chandrakant has moved far away from his humble beginnings as the son of a textile store clerk in the arid wastes of Kutch. With his penchant for Alfa Romeos, original Husains and gold monogrammed Havanas which he holds rakishly awry, he is one of the sauve, emancipated nouveau riche, the type that does not relish telling the world that he is a self-made man.

He is much happier talking in his loud American accent of the woe that is his life as a millionaire. "I am never allowed to live in peace. Last month I had to suddenly rush off to Stockholm—my Swedish collaborators—next week it is to New York, a trade delegation this time," Chandrakant affably complains at your first meeting. "As I was telling Charat Babu—our new commerce minister—if you keep pushing me around so much who is going to look after my group of industries?"

The Marriage Train

Actually it was a trip abroad that initially helped to catapult Chandrakant into the rarefied world of the rich. Twenty years ago he had gone to America to study engineering with the help of a loan. Upon his return he contrived to have his picture published in a local daily along with a little write-up felicitating him on his numerous, if somewhat exaggerated achievements abroad. It was a cue for the marriage train. Soon a machinery of Brahmins, brokers, horoscopewallas and fathers of marriageable daughters were knocking at his door.

Chandrakant selected Usha. She was no apsara to look at but her father was prepared to compensate him with a flat, a car and a substantial share in the family business.

Usha had been to university but after her marriage to a "foreign-returned" felt the need to improve her English which she did by attending a conversation class run by one of the embassies in town. She is now a cool and collected memsaheb tastefully dressed in French chiffons and is articulate as a committee member of an institute for destitute widows.

Chandrakant and Usha are a happy couple, proud of their elegant home which has been photographed for a women's weekly, and of their children, who have been to convent schools and

consequently speak English with the correct accent.

Then there is the parvenu—the not so polished or educated variety of nouveau riche, the type that forms a leitmotif for every satire on the subject.

To look at, Surajmal is like a dictionary illustration of the term. He exudes a flavour of scented hair oils and rich spicy foods. He has a round shining face, neon-lit smile and plump, ringed hands.

Surajmal is inclined to be indulgent in his taste. His bungalow, vaguely modern in design, is furnished in the best tradition of a Hindi film set. It has Moorish room dividers, a Sanchi gateway done in red plaster of Paris, Formica panelled walls, candy pink sofas in resplendent satin, violently flowered curtains and vast portraits of varied gods and goddesses.

Entertaining is a ritual with Surajmal. Government officials must from time to time be appeased if licences have to be obtained. A feast that would do credit to a maharajah is always laid out upon these occasions, for Surajmal is a lavish host. He is therefore pained when his invitations are spurned by some of the dapper executives of foreign commercial firms, companies he could buy up overnight.

For all his *joie de vivre* at his parties Surajmal is relaxed only in the company of his old buddies, childhood friends who have not done so well in life. He rarely grudges their requests for favours, for it is they, with their rapt attention to his bombasts and their eagerness to please, who give him the sense of security he so often finds lacking in the outside world.

Shuklabai, his wife, has no place in Surajmal's socialising. He is embarassed by her peasant ways and her betel-stained gold teeth. But he is proud of his daughters-in-law, tall strapping girls whom he has handpicked not because of their dowry, but because of their light skin.

Mammon and Venus

Every nouveau riche man wants to live like the Gaekwars, to send his sons to Michigan, to become a member of Willingdon Club, if only to experience through it the sense of rubbing shoulders with an exclusive set.

The urge to establish social superiority manifests itself in many ways. Sometimes it is expressed in vainglorious gestures of entertaining burra sahebs and members of the diplomatic corps, reluctant guests who have to be wooed with Chivas Regal. Sometimes it is through vast donations to the Red Cross if only for the sake of being mentioned in the social columns of fashion magazines. Sometimes it is in possessing a fleet of Ford Mustangs and perhaps even a Beach Craft Bonanza. But almost always this irrepressible desire for social heights is stimulated by an adolescent wish fulfilment, a longing to be accepted into the exclusive fold. The sybaritic sophistication of the old nobility, by seeming inexorably out of reach only gives greater validity to all endeavours to Belong.

A WEDDING TO ORDER

THOUGH I HAD FORGOTTEN the card, I remembered the address as Acharya Jagdish Marg. Alas! Acharya Jagdish Marg had more weddings than we had bargained for. Every second building greeted us with the same garishly painted cardboard arches and a loud crescendo of film music. We tried an entrance, and were joyously greeted by a large phalanx of richly caparisoned relatives. We gushed back with our bonhomie and proceeded towards the glittering bridal couple smothered in garlands. But they were not the couple we knew; we beat an ignoble retreat.

Our third attempt brought luck. The bride's family were reassuringly familiar. As at the other receptions, there were same mock-Doric pillars, marigold-beaded arches, rotating neon-lights, liveried waiters, and guests tucking into the same brand of ice-cream. Even the harassed photographer was part of the standard equipment.

We mentioned our earlier tribulations to our host. He chuckled affably. The similarity everywhere was understandable, he said, because the same caterer served the entire locality. "He is a most accommodating chap," said our host. "When we fixed the wedding date, there was no place available to hold the reception. Then along came Mr. Haridas and fixed everything up! Of course, we must vacate the premises by eight o'clock." He anxiously consulted his watch. "There is another reception scheduled for eight-thirty in this place".

"What happens if your guests stay on?" I couldn't resist asking.

"Mr. Haridas gives 15 minutes grace and then switches off the lights." We are impressed that an entire army of relatives can be dismissed by merely the pressing of a button.

"Yes, yes!" chimes our host enthusiastically. "Mr Haridas is a real social worker. His new 'Wedding Package Deal' is a real boon to people. Now they can get married first and pay for the expenses in monthly instalments."

By now Mr. Haridas has joined us. "What if the couple get a divorce before completing their payment?" I asked. "Well," explains Mr. Haridas with grave discretion, "I calculate that a marriage breaks up because one or both of the partners want to marry again. Therefore, I have put in a clause in my contract which stipulates that I am to receive the entire catering order for the new wedding. So, one way or another, I am safe. Actually, with divorces becoming common, business is rather good."

Mr. Haridas elaborates on his services. Over and above the staples like food, drink and decoration, he is in a position to provide a live band, a Brahmin priest for the ceremony, and a flower-decked convertible. Mr. Haridas's resourcefulness leaves us speechless. I wondered whether having so adequately equipped the wedding party, would the inexhaustible Mr. Haridas also provide a hired bride in an emergency to avoid disappointing the guests?

In a crisis, a bride in a traditional palki can be produced.

While desolation had descended upon old Chinatown after the 1962 border war, a smaller Chinese community continued to thrive. Chinese restaurants did roaring business and the famous paper Dragon Races glided through the town every year amidst the bursting of fire crackers!

Choonghee Dong Thien Haue Chinese Church.

A sketch of Chinatown by Desmond Doig.

India's only Mandarin newspaper is still being published.

Chinese breakfast at Tiretta Bazaar is an institution by itself, and popular to this day.

Chinese shoemakers are still popular.

CHINATOWN, CALCUTTA: 1972

The Illustrated Weekly of India, December 17, 1972

CHINATOWN WAS ONCE A forbidden exotic world pocked with opium dens. Today a pucca road has stripped it of its mystery and, after the Chinese invasion, one out of every four of its citizens have left. This is the story of those who remained.

There was a time when the highest concentration of the community in India was in a pocket of Calcutta called Chinatown. A maze of narrow lanes, flanked by dingy houses piled hugger-mugger alongside, often malodorous and lit by gas, Chinatown had a legend of its own.

It was the symbol of the forbidden and the exotic, of the squalid with flashes of the opulence of Far Cathay—claustrophobic and yet fascinating. Chinatown reflected a Somerset Maugham world—sinister, full of surprises and a bizarre splendour. The gaslight jostling with the incense of joss-sticks flung subterranean shadows as slit-eyed men silently glided through dark streets. Bustling cafes belched aromatic vapours of chop suey and dimsum. Colourful shops displayed a multitude of wares from exquisite statues of Confucius and carved ivory chopsticks to pickled snails and egg tarts.

Much of this has gone now—swept away with the rubble of the past. Chinatown, which once had a Chinese population of 20,000, can now barely claim 4,000, most of its inhabitants having left in the wake of the 1962 war. Many of the old buildings musty and rheumatic with age, have also gone—demolished under the hammer blows of the Calcutta Improvement Trust. Vast skyscrapers have thundered up against the skyline, dwarfing the famous Sea Ip Temple, its jade-green tiled roof, rakishly crowned by delicate porcelain fishes, seeming strangely forlorn in this modern jungle of asphalt and steel.

A restaurant famous for its Peking Duck, and stylish still in spite of its peeling paint, has lost much of its old clientele. Behind the swing doors of a roulette den a few old men silently ruminate over a game of dice.

Whereas desolation has descended upon old Chinatown, life for the Chinese community is far from dead in Calcutta. In South Tangra, only four miles away, life surges with a populace of 6,000 Chinese—young, old immensely hard-working. Leather is big business here and the air is ripe with the odour from the tanneries. Along the winding road which runs through its middle—its marching file of dull brick houses displaying notices in Chinese—one comes across a clump of women in boiler suits (one with a bright-eyed child slung on her back) chirping like birds. In open spaces on the roadside, men in large straw hats crouch quaintly, stretching the hides to dry.

There are now 15,000 Chinese in India, 12,500 of whom live in Calcutta. The great exodus took place soon after the 1962 war, when about 8,000 people were deported to Deoli Camp in Rajasthan and later sent back to Mainland China; a vast majority of these being Chinese seamen. Many others also left in the uneasy disquiet of war, fearing that a surge of patriotism might jeopardize their business.

In the last ten years, the Chinese in India have been permitted to continue unhindered in their trades. Five hundred people of Chinese origin, it is reported, have been granted Indian nationality. The rest are required to possess Certificates of

Identity. A few Mainland China passport-holders linger in the country. But their numbers are dwindling. They are prohibited all official links with Mainland China. Until recently, the Choong Kok School in Bow Bazar, Calcutta, used to be run by them. At one time, it accommodated 200 students but, with diminishing patronage, the school had to close its doors in June this year.

Peking vs Taiwan

Before the Red Dragon breathed fire and brimstone on our borders, fiery skirmishes used to take place in the Chinese boroughs of the city between the pro-Peking group and the pro-Taiwan group, with the former generally getting the upper hand. In the last decade, the volcanic pro-Peking faction has either fled or lost its spleen.

The majority of Chinese residents in Calcutta came from in and around Canton and speak Cantonese. A sober, hard-working community, they are an enduring, self-denying lot, gifted with a delicacy of touch which puts them among the best craftsmen in the country. Quietly, unostentatiously they go about their daily chores, providing a backbone to many of the smaller but vital trades of the city—leather export and shoe manufacture, dentistry, laundering, hairdressing, catering and carpentry.

Cautious and publicity shy, the Chinese are a little wary of being drawn into the limelight. Nevertheless, to the stranger who cares to venture in their midst, they are warm and welcoming. They take pains to impress upon him their ties with the country of their domicile. "We love Indian food and often cook it in our homes," they proudly state. "We love Indian films too. Waheeda Rehman and Rajesh Khanna are our favourites!"

It is true. The Chinese journal of India, a four-page daily printed in Chinese from Calcutta and with a circulation of over 1,000 copies, devotes half a page to advertisements of the latest celluloid extravaganzas from Bombay!

"Indian Government and Indian people are very good to us," says K.C. Yap, President of the pro-Taiwan Chinese Overseas Association which claims to represent over 80 per cent of the Chinese community in India, showing us photographs of himself with Mr. Nehru and Mrs. Gandhi. Their community suffers from no discrimination from the Government even after the 1962 war. The proprietor of a large leather business in South Tangra says: "The STC allows us to compete on equal terms with any other Indian firm for the export market."

Suspects

Nevertheless certain restrictions have been imposed on the movement of the Chinese. "We are under survey of the Security Department. We cannot be absent from our homes for more than 24 hours without official permission," says Y.S. Tham, Vice-President of the same organization. "Mr. Nehru and Mr. Chiang Kai-shek were great personal friends. But alas! we are sometimes made to feel like suspects, even though we have always had the most affectionate ties with India."

The restrictions on movement have led to some rather tragic-comic situations. One of the prescribed rules is that residents of the Calcutta Metropolitan District cannot venture into 24-Parganas without prior permission. Now rules are rules and they must be observed. But what happens when a certain street, well populated by the Chinese, forms the boundary line between these two districts? Residents can only cross at the risk of being clamped into prison!

Pei May Chinese school, then and now.

A sense of alienation has crept into the community, leading to a slow but steady migration, particularly of the young and well qualified. Twenty-four-year-old Chen Yuan Chang studied International Trade at the National Chengchi University in Taipeh and now teaches at the Pei Mey School in South Tangra. But he is not at ease here. "What future is there for us now? The big commercial firms hesitate to employ us. All we can do is start our own business. A great many of my colleagues have settled in Canada and the US and they have good jobs there."

There is brisk and bountiful business, however, for those in their own trades. Chinese is taught as three schools in Calcutta. English is the Second Language and Hindi is compulsory. The largest of these schools, Pei Mey, has 450 students, 22 teachers and goes up to Standard IX.

Pei Mey School claimed a strength of over 1,000 students only a decade ago. Many of its older pupils have now settled abroad but not all of them wish to migrate. Twenty-year-old Kuerhsien Yap, who spent two years in Taiwan studying Chinese Language and is about to proceed to the States to do Law, is quite clear in his mind that he wishes to settle in India which he feels is his real home. Born and brought up in Calcutta, he loves rosogollas and puchkas (pani-puri) and will happily queue up overnight for an IFA Shield football match.

The majority of Chinese are Buddhists. There are a few hundred Christians and about 40 Muslims. A handful professes to have no religion; presumably they are Marxists. The Chinese pursue their religions at nine Buddhist temples, two Christian churches and a few small temples devoted to various Chinese gods.

Ancestor worship is an integral part of their lives, no matter what the religious denomination of the individual. Mock replicas of various items that an ancestor is likely to need are made in paper and burnt before the deities: thus symbolically forwarded to the next world.

Chinese temples are ornate and gilded, often decorated with beautiful gold-leaf and camphor-wood carvings. Heavy scarlet awnings sumptuously embroidered with Golden Dragon motifs hang from the ceiling. Before the deity is a huge incese-burner where devotees offer joss-sticks and lighted tapers. Fragrant tea in small bowls is also offered. At the auspicious hour, the caretaker priest rhythmically pounds on a drum with a padded pole, beckoning people to prayer. Most Chinese temples have a god of wealth.

The Chinese in Calcutta have been known to worship the Goddess Kali as well. As a matter of fact, in the twenties, the Blackburn Lane entrance to Chinatown was guarded by a Kali temple which later came to be known as "Cheena Kali" as many Chinese came to offer sacrifices there!

Chinese festivals are all connected with the moon. On these festive occasions, lanterns are hung outside doors and people visit friends. Different delicacies are associated with different festivals: rice cakes for the Dragon feast, moon cakes for the moon festival, spring cakes and sugar dumplings for the New Year.

Paper Dragon—Not Tiger

The famous and traditional Dragon Boat Races have never been held over the Hooghly as they are over the Yangtze. Nevertheless, at the time of the New Year (January-February), massive paper dragons and lions are carried in procession amidst bursting of fire-crackers from Chinatown to South Tangra.

Chinese families are large and patriarchal with strong loyalties which bind the clan together. Forms of good behaviour are precisely etched and implicitly observed. Chinese etiquette is elaborate and fastidious with enough rules to put Emily Post out of business. For instance, it is improper for a Chinaman to wear spectacles in the presence of his superior!

The Chinese attach tremendous dignity to labour. Industrious and thrifty, each member in the family contributes to the running of the household. In factories and workshops, the proprietor works side by side with the labourers. In South Tangra, the son of a wealthy tannery owner feels no squeamishness in tackling the lowliest task in the factory; a foreign-qualified young man, bell-bottomed and wearing go-go glasses; he speaks English with a marked Yorkshire burr. Nevertheless, in the factory, he works on an even keel with the humblest worker.

Gambling with dice, cards, and mahajong are a favourite pastime with the Chinese. Leisure moments are sometimes spent in composing clever antithetical sentences and inscribing them on scrolls to be given away as presents. Pen-and-ink sketches are also made on paper and on fans. Though there is no Chinese theatre in India, schools put up pageants and plays during the festive season.

The Butterfly Dance and the Lantern Dance, with girls dressed in long traditional gowns with flapping sleeves, are popular. The organ seems to be a favourite instrument and is used in all schools. Gongs, cymbals, drums and stringed instruments form a part of the orchestra.

There prevails a vague notion in many minds that the Chinese eat snakes. This is largely untrue. Pork is the chief meat of the Chinese and rice or noodles form a basic part of the daily diet. Vegetables artistically cut and lightly cooked are an integral part of the meal. Meat and fish are cut into pieces and cooked, as the Chinese think it barbaric to carve meat on the table. Besides, food has to be finely chopped so that it can be picked up by chopsticks. A drink of tea generally rounds up the meal.

A piece of raw ginger and fern are hung upon the entrance door of the house in which the baby is born to ward off evil spirits. When a baby boy completes a month, his head is shaved at a special ceremony where prayers are offered at temples and to the ancestral gods. Eggs, dyed red, are distributed among relatives.

The Chinese male has several names; he keeps his surname throughout his life but at every memorable event he acquires a new name. The surname always comes first. A month after a child is born he is given a "milk name" which clings to him all his life. On going to school he is given a "book name". On marriage he acquires a "great name", and, on embarking on a career, the "official name". After death, the individual is known by his "posthumous name" in the hall of his ancestors.

Marriages, by and large, are still "parent-arranged". The betrothal is negotiated by a go-between. The horoscope is first examined by an astrologer, and then presents of tea, cakes, betel-nut and money wrapped up in red paper are made to the bride's parents. When these are officially accepted, the daughter is declared betrothed. In Canton a bride used to be carried in a red ornamental chair, ornately carved, and was accompanied by a clashing of gongs to her groom's house.

In our present bread-and-butter age, the Chinese bride is driven in a flower-decked car to her future home, where the celebrations are held. The bridal couple offer prayers to the ancestral gods and to the parents-in-law. No dowry is paid for a girl. On the contrary, the boy's parents must give lavish presents to secure a good bride for their son! Over the bridal bed are hung long strips of paper containing good wishes like "May you have 100 sons and 1,000 grandsons!" the bridal couple play games to decide who will have the upper hand in later life!

The Chinese are very particular in the observance of the rituals of mourning. Mourners are clothed in coarse white sack-cloth, while sons and nearest of kin wear caps of the same material. White lanterns are hung at the gate. If the man leaves behind a widow, she and her children sit on the ground for seven days and sleep near the coffin. No food is cooked in the house for a week. Interestingly, a Chinese is required to wear mourning for his superiors and equals but not necessarily for his wife!

The body is kept embalmed in the house for a period of two to seven days. At an auspicious day and time, the body is taken out in an elaborate procession to the cemetery amidst chanting of prayer and burning of incense and candles. There is a Chinese saying which goes: "The most important thing in life is to get buried well."

New year celebrations in Chinatown remain a colourful, joyous affair!

A TEA PLANTER'S LIFE

Tea plantations in northeast India were remote and offered a completely different way of life.

A sketch of a typical "Burra Bungalow." Courtesy: Goodrickes

The Planters wives: Ready for a hunt or a ball.

A planter attending to daily business. He also dealt with the problems of his workers as their 'mai-baap'.

TEA PLANTER: A MAN FOR ALL SEASONS

The Statesman, July 1, 1979

Mr. X was a planter near Tinsukhia, Upper Assam. One January morning this year, he had an unusual visitor at the factory office.

"Very nice meeting you, Mr. X," said the courteous guest, a man sentenced to life for murder but who had escaped prison in a few months. He now collected 'subscriptions'. He said, "I have a small request. I shall be grateful if you will be good enough to keep Rs. 50,000 ready in cash this afternoon. I shall call again at 4 p.m. Do keep this transaction between ourselves After all you do have a wife and children you wish to protect." To emphasise his point the visitor made a sudden karate chop making the heavy table quake like jelly. The moment passed. He was once again the affable urbane visitor. A smile and a nod and he sauntered out.

Few planters are called upon to face such a situation. Nevertheless, life in the wilds can hold many surprises and dangers. The planter learns to move with the confidence of a leader, proud of the long tradition he is upholding, retaining his calm amidst all recriminations and threats, sympathetic, and yet unemotional. He takes many things in his stride—demolishing a nest of cobras unexpectedly found outside the baby's nursery window, chasing up a maneater, or serving as a father confessor to his brood. The planter is a tough man, endlessly resourceful, and also a master of the art of downing innumerable chota pegs!

To the outsider, the planter's world seems to be an exotic place familiar to us through the works of Somerset Maugham and Joseph Conrad; a legend kept alive by the tropical extravaganzas from Hollywood.

However evocative, these are illusions. Certainly, there was a time in the early part of the century when many of these fantasies bordered on fact. The whiskered, hunter-swishing planter in his solar topee and white ducks, autocratic perhaps, but accepted as omniscient, could well have been true. His abode was a veritable mansion, flanked by a tennis-court and smothered in a riot of bougainvillea, and filled with lofty high-ceilinged rooms and echoing Kafkaesque recesses, tended to by an endless army of servants. It was then the age of polo and shikar with His Excellency, of chota hazri under a striped canopy over a manicured lawn, of hostesses languishing over 'station gup'; of afternoon gin sessions at the club lengthening into a hazy, sullen night.

That was the time when, at a special coming-of-age party, the planters drove to their destination all formally attired, their ladies a vision in satin and lace. The band and the chef for the occasion were imported from Firpos of Calcutta and a small army of "jee-hazoor"-ing house-boys assiduously polished the dance floor for 30 days to make the ball the talk of the district for years to come.

It was a life of prerogative and position, of benevolent despotism juxtaposed with immense toil and stamina to survive the malaria and black fever and the untold dangers of a merciless tropical jungle. That was a life when a 'polo pony allowance' was among the essential prerequisites granted to a young assistant manager and it was *de rigeur* for the superintendent of gardens to have a private staff of 20 domestics.

All this is now part of history. The old clubs, once subsisting solely on the fancies and the peccadillos of the planter, now look withdrawn and derelict; the paint peeling behind the bar and the waiters' uniforms stained with remnants of countless forgotten meals. A great backwash of modernity has swept over the world and society has changed under the impact of liberal ideas; moved far from the stage when the manager was the monarch of all he surveyed and his worker a chattel; each taking the other's lot as destined and irrevocable. The pomp and the circumstance has gone but not, alas, the memories. The privileges, the prerogatives have departed, but the illusions of unalloyed prosperity and creature comforts remain, and these are what churn up resentment in the outside world.

To understand, one should look at the *raison d'être* of a planter's calling. Growing and manufacturing tea is only part of his job. His is a lonely existence. Sometimes his nearest neighbour is 30 miles away. The children have to be sent to a boarding school and life away from near and dear ones is often chilly and forlorn. A planter could well ruminate, Alexander Selkirk-like, "Oh, Solitude, where are the charms that sages have seen in thy face?" The roads are not always pukka or traversable by car. In times of landslides or floods, all communications are snapped and he is metaphorically marooned on an island, isolated from the world.

The planter's spouse needs all her wits to run a fluid, accommodating home, capable of hosting half a dozen unexpected dinner guests before providing beds for them for the night!

Also, the peace and serenity which seems such a balm to a casual city soul on a visit to the gardens can assume terrifying, brooding proportions in times of unrest. Each trembling shadow on the lawn could be that of a stalking assailant and dangerous.

It is scarcely surprising that the planter has been likened to a captain of a ship. He is his own legal advisor, labour officer and engineer. He is called upon to sit in judgment on his men's most intimate domestic problems: "My wife has run away with my neighbour. Kindly arrange to restore her to me, Sir." The boss's verdict is always accepted as final and sacrosanct. Should a rogue elephant stray into the garden the workers look to their saheb to deal with the beast.

The planter can also be called upon to face the mob ignited by a handful of mischief-makers from outside. Many have displayed astonishing courage on occasion. A planter was once gheraoed by several hundred men. The men closed in to watch with bated breath as their leader threateningly pointed a kukri at the captive's throat. The manager's unflinching response was: "All right, kill me. Or else, get out." The man withdrew.

All this and much more makes the planter what he is—a man for all seasons. If he is sometimes accused of being a brown saheb—more pukka than the original product—so what? There is the odd planter who with his *koi hais* and fussy manners, his passion for his pipe, the *Daily Telegraph* and outdated slang continues to resurrect the Raj in his person. He belongs to a bygone age. Nevertheless, he holds out an affectionate appeal for things past. It is he who adds dimension of colour and nostalgia to what is now a sedate, pragmatic, down-to-earth community.

AN AVANT GARDE EVENING

The Statesman, 11 November, 1979

EVERYWHERE IN THE LARGER cities of India these days people are ardently applying themselves to the pursuit of Culture. The acquisition of *objets d'art* has become the new status symbol of today.

There was a time once when these people happily whiled away a Sunday afternoon at the club playing golf and downing innumerable chota pegs. But alas! Not so since the culture plague has struck, setting off virulent allergies. Now they bravely squeeze themselves into raw silk sherwanis to be seen at the opening of a Polish art exhibition.

Their brisk bridge-playing wives with sculptured hair-dos, who were at one time content to spend countless coffee mornings speculating on whose marriage was heading for the rocks, now sit on committees of literary academies and boast about the latest antique they have acquired.

Even normally sensible people are succumbing to the attack. They all want to go fashionably bohemian. Their favourite literature had hitherto been of the Agatha Christie and Perry Mason order, but now they read Laurence Durrell and T.S. Eliot. Instead of listening to Lata Mangeshkar over Vividh Bharati they listen to concerts of Chamber Music put up by local amateur societies and try to look as though they enjoy them.

In painting they have always subscribed to life-like sketches of familiar objects; perhaps a mother rocking a child to sleep or a pretty maid by a rose bush. But not so now. All this is considered crassly bourgeois. So these are wistfully cast away and replaced by abstracts of tortured symbolism where a human being is dismissed in a couple of triangles and a blob of paint can mean anything from a child to infinity!

Sudhir Dayal is one of the pioneers of the species. Having spent two summers plodding over art galleries in Europe, he considers himself to be a sort of cultural guru. A carefully acquired *presque boheme* air hangs around his person. His clothes are strictly casual. He is bearded and his glasses horn-rimmed. To meet for the first time he can be disconcerting. You must be prepared to submit to his inquisition.

By day Sudhir Dayal is a highly successful banker who goes all cultural by night. For alas! Culture, to sustain, requires finance. It is only fair! An invitation to a Dayal party is a memorable experience peopled with minor poets, painters, architects, movie-makers, critics and young debonaires. The newcomer treads gingerly. The dimly-lit flat is like ye olde curiosity shop, the floor being disturbingly littered with wood-carvings, headless bronzes, vast ceramic ashtrays, folk art cushions and jungles of potted plants.

The guests are gathered around the hostess. Cool and elegant-looking in a hand-printed handloom, Mrs. Dayal wears vast quantities of primitive tribal jewellery around her slim neck. Her eyes are heavily outlined with kohl and in her manicured hand she flourishes a long ivory cigarette holder which is forever catching into things.

She is drawing the attention of her guests to a latest acquisition—a painting depicting what looks like a pink face with green ears supported by a pair of spidery thin legs stretching towards

Illustration for article 'Gay Debonaires' in the Statesman(Jr), June 8, 1968.

the horizon. "Don't you think our new Subhash Vaidya is too-too great for words?" She looks expectantly at the company.

A chorus of ecstatic little cries of appreciation is obediently set off. The newcomer looks blankly. He is reminded of his seven year-old niece's efforts. They could well compete with Subhash Vaidya. "But, what is it supposed to mean?" he ventures innocently.

The guests wince as though their credulity has been strained. "Mean?" snaps the hostess flashing him a look of withering disdain. "Why should it have a meaning? It is in the meaninglessness that lies the meaning."

"And now folks, 1 simply cannot wait for you to see our Nataraj." She briskly shepherds her flock to a large and crippled bronze. "Looks kinda real old," says the American guest.

"Isn't it!" gushes Mrs. Dayal. "I was assured it is a genuine antique dating back to the Chola dynasty. The only way to tell a real genuine Nataraj of this period is this sign. She points out a miniscule heiroglyphic sign. That is what our dealer says. All of the statues of the Chola dynasty discovered so far have this sign!" she finishes authoritatively.

"And now what do you think of this?" she asks, holding for inspection a crude, chipped blue earthenware bowl.

"The texture has a marvellous earthy, primitive, barbaric appeal," the minor poet promptly chimes.

Mrs. Dayal smiles triumphantly. "Should we let them into our secret Sudhir?" she coyly appeals across the room to her husband who is half reclining on a low diwan made up of bits of carved wood. He wears a pink Lucknawi kurta and is smoking a hookah. He smiles back indulgently.

"This bowl is a fake!" gleefully announces the wife. When the cries of, "Well, I never ..." have died down, Mrs. Dayal continues, "We know this clever little man who specialises in giving the right antique touch. By the by, he is particularly good with Rajasthani miniatures. He fades the colours so well that when he has finished you can hardly tell what the painting is all about. Isn't that just great?"

The newcomer edges to the door. But not before he can escape her admonishing scrutiny. "Tut, tut," Mrs. Dayal wags a playful finger at her errant guest. "You cannot possibly go off just yet. Why, you haven't even heard Sudhir's poems."

"What, does he write too?" asks the newcomer trying to conceal his dismay.

"He is no T.S. Eliot," she proudly confesses. "But one of his poems was recently published in the *Honolulu Chronicle*."

The guests turn expectantly to their host. He pulls out a wad of notes from his pocket, clears his throat and says, "Well, this is not my best but if you insist."

The poem sounds like a soulful lament on the dead. There is repeated reference to the canine species and just as the newcomer is surmising it to be a requiem on a pet dog, it transpires that the poet is referring to human beings. It is all very confusing but the newcomer now knows that the more obscure a work the greater the likelihood of it being accepted as art.

Appreciative comments arrow through the air, with the gay young ladies taking the lead. It is an impressive statement on modern civilisation, says the minor poet. The 'double symbolism' appeals to the American guest. Someone praises it for its 'delicate sensitivity', another thinks it is the 'clever satire' which makes it great. But they all agree it is a profund little piece and express pain at the knowledge that the poem has not been hitherto published.

Sudhir Dayal acknowledges the compliments graciously. "Hullo there!" he says spotting the newcomer.

"I… think your poem is very good," stammers the newcomer wretchedly, feeling trapped.

"Well, one tries," says Sudhir Dayal with a deprecating little gesture. "Our life is so hollow and mechanised. Don't you find it so? I always long to get away from it. And poetry is my escape valve. Now enough about myself. What about you? Do you do anything creative?

"Not paint or anything like that? Well I suppose you immerse yourself in all the challenging things happening in town. All the good shows and things. What did you think of Martha Plywood's Modern Ballet?"

"I must confess I haven't been able to see it. Got rather involved in the office.'

"What about Professor Niranjan Das's lectures on 'Mystic Symbols in Greek Philosophy'?" continues the inquisition.

"Surely you could not have missed those. What? No time? I suppose then you did not have time for that rather surrealistic new Japanese film either," the voice is now heavy with sarcasm. "I suppose you'd much rather spend an evening with James Bond, wouldn't you now?

"Well, my dear young man, I am afraid," says the culture guru, "I am afraid we hold little appeal for you. We clearly ascribe to a different wave-length."

"Why is he thinking? Did he lose his smartphone?"

THE BRIGHTEST STARS

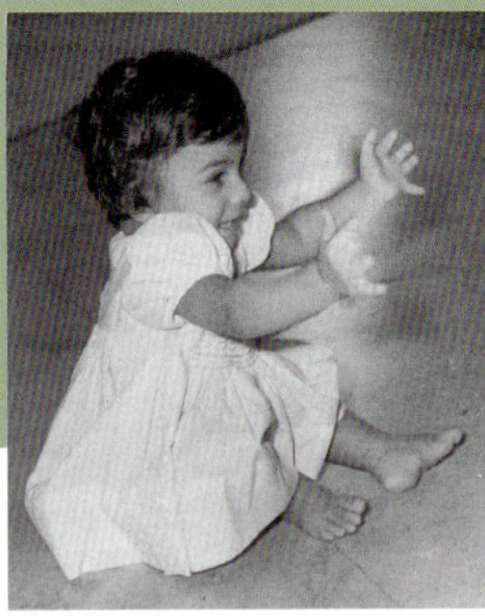

Madhavi

Brinda

The sisters ready to party!

On holiday in Europe.

At home in Calcutta.

A MUMMY'S BRAIN

The Statesman, January 18, 1979

We were in London on holiday. But before our departure I had casually let it be known that I was also planning to nip across to the British Museum to do a spot of research. It had sounded charmingly dilettantish, investing the trip with a refinement far beyond the usual round of brutish pleasure. There was only one major snag: our travelling companions in this instance were our two daughters, aged eight and twelve. "How will you manage with them?" a cynical friend had asked. "All a question of organisation," was my lofty dismissal.

It had seemed simple enough. A judicious blend of appeal and bribery should have sufficed. We would treat them to a hectic merry-go-round of London. And there would be the occasional afternoons when they, in turn, would nobly consent to sitting around in the museum foyer while I did a bit of work.

I had dainty little visions of my poring over a rare manuscript while the girls sat demurely outside, engrossed in their favourite Enid Blytons and dreaming of teatime with the promised chocolate cake and ice-cream.

All goes well in the beginning, as things generally do. The girls are as good as gold and eight-year-old Madhavi does not take out her crayons to decorate the walls. Instead she makes friends with the benign hall-porter on duty. The sessions in the library are also satisfying. The average age of the readers, on that particular occasion, was well above 60 and, as a consequence, I was subjected to flattering male attention. I feel I am once again a slip of a student aspiring to be a scholar. The young librarian readily offers to track down rare reference material and, when he fails, a hidden professor bobs up from behind a bookshelf proferring help. They listen to my fumbling and somewhat Utopian research plans with suitable graveness. Their interest is very touching, sweetly making me forget that I am a parent of two, with straggly eyebrows and thoughts wandering to unfinished homework and parent-teacher meetings.

Alas! as though to prohibit these unmotherly feelings a grizzled porter rushes in to whisper that Madhavi is missing. One moment she was sitting quietly chewing gum and the next she had disappeared.

Mummies on display at the British Museum.

I jump up, knocking back the chair. The crash sounds like sacrilege in this hushed parlour. But my only thought is to find the missing child.

Several hall porters join in the search. We rush up the wide staircase and down miles of the museum's corridors. Centuries of history pass by. Neither the armless Greek goddesses nor their urns yield the child. We zoom around the Aztec double-headed serpent mosaic and cabinets of broken Chinese pottery.

Madhavi is finally tracked down in the Egyptian section. It is eerie there with the silent rows of mummies swathed in bandages. She is reading with considerable interest the ancient recipe of the pharaohs for making mummy-filling preservatives. The gory details are all given: first remove the brain, next mix it up with extracts from the liver....

Madhavi turns and fixes me a glance of prickling intensity. Sternly she says, "Mummy, now I know what people in Egypt do to their Mummy's brains."

CHARTER OF DEMANDS

The Statesman, May 5, 1979

Our 12-year-old Brinda comes home from school and announces that she has been asked to make a historical chart on the French Revolution. And it must have illustrations.

Chart-making is doubtless excellent exercise for children. From a mother's point of view, however, it can have less desirable implications. For me, it means sending urgent summons to grandpa for advice, sympathy and consolation. It means my popping my head into the nearest *Encyclopedia Britannica* to catch up on Marie Antoinette and the Reign of Terror. It also means scouting around for grisly details such as the daily output of an eighteenth-century guillotine. "Please Mummy," enjoins Brinda, "just imagine how much more colourful this information will make my chart".

It means ransacking the attic for that suitcase containing newspaper cuttings and picture post-cards for possible illustrations. It means bringing the household to a grinding halt as servants are sent off to get chart-paper, gum, colour pencils, cellophane, gold trimming and other such items of embellishment. The notion that parenthood is a shared joy proves untrue at times like this. Fathers, I feel, have a premonition about chart-producing days. They invariably have a sick colleague to visit or a business contact to meet which prevents them from coming to your aid.

When at last the equipment has been assembled and the text prepared, Brinda spreads herself out on the dining table, with the whole family, including the servants, standing around in reverential silence. For a long moment she closes her eyes in deep and silent meditation. Then with slow deliberation she picks up her pen, dips it into the ink-well, makes a sweeping, experimental gesture in the air, lowers it over the chart paper and drops a large blob of ink in the centre. "Now look at that!" she wails in the tones of one more sinned against than sinning. The stain resists all rubbing with the eraser and a greasy thumb.

A new sheet is fetched. By now a power-cut has begun so somebody is appointed to hold a torch, another to read out the text, a third to guard the bottle of ink and a fourth to pass the colour pencils. Almost half the written work is over when it is discovered that the illustrative picture postcards are missing. "Where on earth are my postcards? What have you all done to my postcards?" Brinda fixes us with an accusing eye. We grope in the dark, looking under tables and fumbling in drawers, until Brinda remembers that she has herself put them in her schoolbag. "It's all right," she says graciously. "Wasn't it clever of me to store them away safely? Otherwise where would we be now?"

Everything goes smoothly until we come to the storming of the Bastille. Nobody seems to remember the exact date. Somebody says it was July 4, another November 14. Brinda says how can we expect her to do well in school when her own family is so blank. The remark is only fair.

By 10 o'clock the lights are back and the chart is ready. Surprisingly it looks neat and attractive. Everybody is worn-out and ready to collapse except Brinda and her father who has just returned home. He surveys our handiwork of toil, tears and sweat and says proudly, "Now didn't I always maintain what a bright little daughter I had?"

THE MAGIC TOUCH

The Statesman, February 27, 1980

OUR YOUNGER DAUGHTER Madhavi, all of nine years old, had a small part as a fairy in her school concert. She looked pretty in the white organdie dress with its tiny silver wings. But alas! on the morning of the concert she broke her cardboard wand into two.

When all use of gum, sticking plaster, scotch tape and choice vituperative language failed to put humpty-dumpty together again Madhavi set up a deafening wail. I had little choice but to resort to immediate professional aid.

At the market the shutters of the birthday decoration and coloured paper store were up though the young proprietor was bleary-eyed with sleep. He deliberated over our broken wand with his grimy fingers and finally pronounced. "Nothing can do here. You go to our factory."

At this juncture the smooth little man in the stall opposite said ingratiatingly, "If you will step this side, madam, I can solve your problem." A practitioner, he could obviously take in the bulge of my bag and the tears on Madhavi's cheeks. No sooner had I stepped into his shop than he said in soothing tones how difficult it was to get silver paper in India anymore. But, he assured me, luck was on my side. He had just one sheet of imported paper in stock. Reverentially he opened it to display a sheet of foil exactly like all the other sheets generally available in Indian markets. He beamed. "Genuine, guaranteed, foreign stuff."

"How much?" I asked.

"For you special price, Rs. 10. For you only," he whispered with a gold-toothed smile.

"It's too much. Leave it," I said getting tired of the fraud.

"Yes, yes, you leave it!" promptly echoed my original birthday decorationwalla from the stall across. He had thought it appropriate now to take a proprietorial interest in my affairs. "Factory," he announced to his competitor. To me he said gently. "I will take you."

He briskly gave directions to the driver to take us to a seedy by-lane in the crowded heart of the city. We stopped before a spare parts shop and he proudly declared, "My uncle Factory!"

On a charpoy in the centre sat a bearded old man in a skullcap, his gnarled hands putting finishing touches to a paper lantern. "My father!" beamed our birthday decorationwalla. The old man welcomed us with a great flourish, took the broken wand, smiled archly at Madhavi and said, "I give you 2-3 minutes. He was as good as his word. Deftly he selected a strip of bamboo, measured it by the eye, cut, smoothed it, selected a strip of silver and rolled it around, pasted it down and handed it back to Madhavi.

"Thank you very much," I said. "Now please tell me how much money I owe you."

I had resigned myself to being taken for a ride. He looked at the notes speculatively, and then to my great surprise, the old man stood up and straightened himself.

"No, madam, no take money today. First time you come to my Factory. Baba, have good party. Baba enjoy, I enjoy."

He then folded his hands.

A CAPTIVE MOTHER

The Hindustan Times, September 20, 1982

THERE COMES A TIME in the life of every mother when she begins to feel harassed, undistinguished and vulnerable.

Brinda, at fifteen, is much more tractable. In the last few weeks she has only made me read *The Tempest*, *Midsummer Night's Dream*, and prepare a five-page essay on the sanitary arrangements of Early Mohenjodaro people. I cannot really complain.

Madhavi, at eleven, is the militant one. She takes me by the scruff of the neck as it were, pulls me inside out, cajoles me, bullies me, forces me to her bidding, making me do things I never meant to do.

Her latest obsession was the school play, in aid of which she went round our house assessing our belongings for their stage potential. She requisitioned several items of furniture before her eye strayed to my wardrobe, coming to rest lasciviously upon an old pink saree which I did not wish to forgo. But my reluctance spurred her determination. I had kept the saree as a sentimental souvenir of my university days overseas—those whirlwind times when I had slogged over James Joyce's *Ulysses* into long, freezing, rheumatic hours of the night while a hissing gas-meter chewed away my precious shillings. A spotty underfed poet had confessed to his being driven to writing a sonnet on the dark-eyed Indian girl when he first saw me wearing that saree. Needless to say, I later discovered that my poet was in the habit of saying this to all the other Indian girls he encountered. They, like me, had also been persuaded to take him out to a tea of hot scones, fresh cream and homemade raspberry jam. Nevertheless, the memory made me feel young and debonaire and I kept the saree as a part of my nostalgia.

Madhavi, age 11.

Madhavi said, "Let me have that saree, Mama. It is only an old one."

Taking my silence for acquiescence, she swiftly volunteered, "I promise to finish my homework in time and not throw clothes on the bathroom floor."

"You cannot have that saree," I said.

"We will be very careful," said Madhavi, pretending not to hear. Refusal had whetted her appetite. "Think of all the goodwill you will earn... of the charities you will be helping." The school concert was supposed to be in aid of sick orphans.

Fear made me passionate and unnecessarily heartless. "No thank you. I can do my own charity," I said.

"What about Papa then?" She cried getting on the offensive, her large black eyes snapping like olives. "It is all very well for you not to care. Is it fair to Papa? I mean to have you wearing this tattered old saree?" She thrust a frayed edge into my face. "What will people in his office say?"

I remained adamant, but Madhavi continued to be inexhaustible. I compromised, letting Madhavi have other sarees, a star-spangled one for herself and one each for all her friends. The pink saree I did not forgo.

Experience should have taught me that the seige would not be abandoned so easily. Sure enough, at dinner that evening Madhavi began her campaign by putting her father at his affable best, asking him to recount the story of the time he scaled his college hostel parapet. She listened round-eyed to this much-heard tale, and as I watched her, I marvelled once again at the Machiavellian traits of all children in general and of little girls in particular. No sooner had he finished, Madhavi said, "Papa, do ask Mummy to let me have her pink saree for my concert. Only you can get it for me."

Flushed with his rip-roaring anecdote and finding himself forced into a position of knight-in-armour, my husband said, "Of course, she will let you have it!" He carefully avoided my eye. Being a parent he knew what it was to have another parent transgress normal rules of discipline. "We will buy Mummy another one," he promised.

"A blue one," said Madhavi giving me a ravishing smile. "Pink does not suit Mummy."

A BIRTHDAY TO REMEMBER

The Times of India, October 21, 1979

I AM IN THE MIDST of a long-due cleaning session of the children's room. Among the dead wood, I happen to come across a broken pink plastic whistle.

Our younger daughter, Madhavi, had received it as a present from one of Mother Teresa's children at Shishu Bhavan in Calcutta almost three years ago. I am immediately reminded of that happy rumbustious hour.

Madhavi was four when we had taken her to Shishu Bhavan, a place which did not at first sight, present an exuberant scene. In the spacious first-floor dormitory was a row of metal cribs. In each crib lay a forlorn little waif, sometimes howling for a mother it would never know. In incubators were the premature babies, shrunken, shrivelled beings with sunken eyes: seeming corpses before they were dead.

Romping in and around the cots were the older children; one with sore-infested limbs, another with the vacant eyes and drooping chin of the retarded. But these children played with gay abandon, oblivious to the cruel and turbulent world outside that had chosen to forget them.

We watched Madhavi make her way through them, clutching the large bag of sweets she had brought for distribution. Spying the goodies, the children stopped indulging in what seemed to be like a merry civil war and made a beeline for the newcomer. Getting within touching distance they however, formed an orderly circle. They then waited politely but expectantly for the next move.

Madhavi now decided to hold a quick consultation. The nearest heads came down together in a conclave as the finer points of peaceful distribution were dissected. The preliminary round over, the bag was swiftly emptied, the numbers counted and divided into lots. "Stand in a line all of you," shouted a self-styled leader. The circle rapidly uncoiled into a straight line. "Put your right hand out!"

The operations were in full swing when the distributors made an alarming discovery. The queue of recipients was continuing to stretch in a never-ending line with stocks dwindling rapidly. Tapus, the master of ceremonies, quickly ran a sharp eye-over the assembly. Like a seasoned customs' official, he then swooped down on the tightly-closed left fist of one imp standing demurely for her turn. She let out a screech. Three sweets fell out of the greasy palm. The curly-haired culprit tried to look suitably repentant, failing which, she gave a disarming, puckish smile.

The fun continued for well over an hour. When it was time to go home, we put a question to Madhavi. Would she, this year, forgo her usual birthday treat at home to let her new friends at

Shishu Bhavan enjoy a party instead? It had to be either one or the other. The choice, however, was strictly hers. Madhavi readily opted to forgo a party at home.

Three years have passed since. Getting onto seven, Madhavi is now a veteran party-goer. Increasing years have bred a blaseness. No more frilly dresses with pink satin sashes for her, thank you. Only babies wear them nowadays. And why do mummies have to make such a fuss about having gas-filled balloons at parties? The cake for her next party is to be, kindly note, shaped like Cinderella's pumpkin coach. And, of course, there must be a mini Gogia Pasha magic show to round-off the party. How can it be called a legitimate birthday otherwise?

I think a little wistfully of that other party at Shishu Bhavan. Had Madhavi completely forgotten her friends? How much had she understood of the spirit of giving? That it was not merely a question of buying a bag of sweets and distributing them. That it was a question of sharing—a parting, with something of one's own to bring happiness to someone else? Or was hers merely an impulsive response to the infectious joyousness of the place? Perhaps her memories of past birthdays were yet vague and fleeting and had not crystallised into a tangible forsaking of candles and cake and a cartload of presents.

These thoughts chase my mind as I open a generally unused bottom desk-drawer. A sickeningly sweet smell stings the air. I gingerly push aside the small bundle of comics on top. Hidden underneath is an enormous pile of the much-coveted sweet bags; the variety ritually given to each child-guest at the end of a birthday party. The collection before me seems to have been gathered over a considerable period. Time and weather have conspired to disintegrate their contents. The outer paper has decomposed but not so totally as to unable me to decipher Madhavi's little scrawl on every bag. It says: "For Mother Teresa's Child."

Mother Teresa with one of her many 'children'.

Cutting the birthday cake!

WILL YOU MARRY ME?

The Illustrated Weekly of India, August 12, 1970

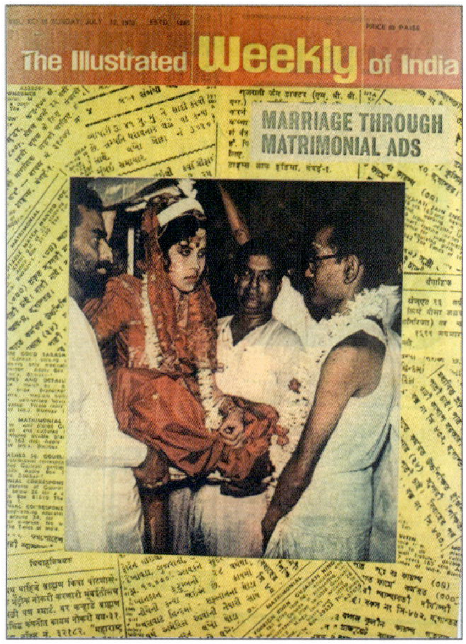

An advertisement in the matrimonial column reads: "Wanted a foreign-returned Hindu young man, executive in British firm, for a really pretty, fairly coloured, soft-spoken, convent-educated girl of 155 cms, well up in cooking, flower-arrangements and meritorious in interior decoration, belonging to a respectable, well-placed family of artistic taste. Father owning two houses in Calcutta promises an early and decent marriage!"

Such an ad has all the ingredients of universal appeal. The girl's convent education ensures an ability to speak English with the right accent and a manner befitting a chota memsahib that would be an asset for a man with a career. To make her proficient in cooking is the quickest way of worming into a mother-in-law's heart, the fair skin a useful stick to silence relatives, and last, but not least, the father's promise of a decent marriage clearly hints that a good dowry is forthcoming. Why mention two houses unless one is for the son-in-law?

In return the girl's family only ask that he be a 'foreign-returned', a qualification which reassures them that his family are rich and emancipated enough to send him abroad for studies and so his chances of succeeding in a British oil company are better than most.

Some years ago the matrimonial advertisements were full of seductions, all encased in asbestos platitudes. The male protagonists in the market were Greek gods, veritable Apollos with aquiline noses and noble brows, of an aristocratic heritage, who, due to worldly reasons, were forced to spend their days working as lecturers and Central Government JCOs. The ladies on the shelves were, one and all, fair young virgins, exquisite ornaments of gilt-and-plush homes, unimpeachable sati Sitas.

Gone are those days, alas, of golden boys and girls. Sceptics have infiltrated the ranks of readers. Like the Upanishadic Svetaketu they are sitting up to ask: WHY? Why should an eligible Bharadwaj-Brahmin boy earning a salary of four figures have to advertise five times in two weeks for a bride? Surely something must be wrong.

'A jug of wine' not enough

The hint is being taken. The young government officer knows that to get a good match he must offer an inducement over and above his physical and metaphysical attributes. So he adds a cunning little clause to his suit—'free living quarters'. Love is all very well so long as there is a roof overhead. Urban housing being the problem it is, he knows that this will improve chances in his favour. For a discerning modern girl a jug of wine and a loaf of bread will not alone suffice.

The B.A., B.T. Kayastha Bose lady teacher confessing her age to be 32 refuses to wander alone while dreaming of a Vishva Bharati professor in shining armour to claim her hand. She is prepared to settle down with 'at least a graduate'!

A father looking for a Rajput groom for his 25-year-old daughter asks only that he be 'distinguished-looking', making no inquiry on his capacity to earn the bread of the family. He frankly admits that his child is 'medium-coloured' but is quick to add as compensation that she is also 'income-drawing'. Besides, Rajput morale being at a low ebb today it is tacitly implied that any extra addition to the family treasury should not be spurned.

For all the entertainment they provide to the casual reader and for all their mechanised approach to human relationships these ads are doing a great service to the acute and anguished problem of matrimony. Life in our country continues to be chilly and desolate for our misfits, the childless widower, the cripple, the deaf and the mute. For them there is little or no common ground to meet and make friends with people from the opposite sex. Had it not been for this institution they would have to fall back upon the mercy of rapacious relatives. A blind political worker was able to meet and marry a normal and healthy young school-teacher through an advertisement. Now they are a happy couple blessed with three beautiful children.

For those settled overseas but wishing to retain their Indian identities through marriage to partners from the same social caste and religion there is perhaps no better answer. A former leather-smith from Midnapore, now a prosperous business man in Trinidad, got his four sons happily married through advertisements. But not everyone is lucky in the gamble. A post-graduate student from New York, having advertised for a wife, came down to Calcutta to marry her. Two months later he discovered to his horror that she was dying of leukemia, a fact carefully concealed from him by her family.

Backwash Of Modernity

A great backwash of modernity has swept over the country in recent years. Old taboos are rapidly breaking down and the young are well placed to pick up partners from a wide range of acquaintances at parties and colleges. Ironically, this has created a peculiar form of wariness. Dating is all good fun but when it comes to marriage the majority retreat like little Jack Horners into corners fighting shy of those whom they daily encounter. Perhaps it is familiarity that breeds indifference. Perhaps it is because there is a restless dream for an ideal—everyone wants to be the Made For Each Other couple. Whatever the reason, there is a swelling number of ads in the matrimonial columns in even old uppity newspapers: *The Statesman* runs a regular matrimonial column every Thursday.

Young men want a swinging, good-looking bride, a millionaire father-in-law, and an expense-paid honeymoon round the world. When neither friends nor relatives can produce such a combination, refuge is sought in advertising. Putting it down in print ensures that the plea will be jet-propelled through space and heard in a thousand homes, one of which, who knows, may turn up with an answer to one's prayers. Good luck to them.

BALLYGUNGE BLUES

The Times of India, April 24, 1983

Now that we are in the process of moving out of Calcutta, I am filled with a heightened longing for that glorious, decadent, rheumatic, esoteric city which to me is hauntingly beautiful. Its quaint snobberies and outdated protocol add a dimension of piquancy so alien to Bombay and Delhi.

Eighteen years ago, I had first come to Calcutta to set up home. After the brisk, pragmatic, neon-lit opulence of Bombay, it had seemed a bewildering world. My husband then worked for a commercial house with a British label which meant that though the Raj may have departed, but the occasional hangover lingered. The pucca memsahibs had already sailed back home on the P & O to the nitty gritty of a home in Tunbridge Wells, and an elderly charwoman. The sahebs had lingered on living out their last days of splendour in lavish bungalows in Ballyunge, Tollygunge and Alipore, stiffened by the hierarchy of khansamas, bawarchis, chowkidars, malis, jamadars, masalchis, and the chokra boy.

Raj Relics

In clubs hearty, pipe-smoking brown sahebs, their names shortened to the closest English equivalent, downed chota pegs. Here again were colonial interiors—lofty rooms with high ceilings and echoing corridors where soft speaking servants silently flitted around. On the walls were portraits of Queen Elizabeth and her Consort at the Coronation, and sporting prints of dashing young men at a pig-sticking spree. At the bar a stiff abdar measured out his chota pegs as an occasional 'koi hai?' whizzed through the air.

Everybody was painfully kind to me as I was new and uninitiated. But it is now easy to see that I must have presented a bit of problem; I was difficult to categorise. Not being from Calcutta I had no easily available reassuring details of a background to present. Nor had I a vast ancestral estate tucked away across the country to support me. Besides, my foreign university education could have hardly helped. The surroundings did not seem to set particular store by blue stockings. Higher education for young women was not so important. They were generally supposed to have fathers well placed enough to enable them to take their own pick of dashing young executives entitled to a good company flat.

Our first home in Calcutta was in a rambling manor belonging to a zamindar. We occupied the first floor; the landlord lived below. To me the place with its black and white marble chessboard floor and its air of fading splendour brought on memories of Satyajit Ray. Long windswept verandahs, as wide as galleries, ran along the two sides. The living area was surprisingly small, as though the cubicle-like rooms had been built as an afterthought and subsequently squeezed between the verandahs. The bathrooms, a frippery scorned by the landlord, were located a great distance away. Nevertheless, the windows were pure stained glass.

Downstairs, the zamindar resided in rooms designed for courtly entertainment—excessively chandeliered and dwarfed by tall Chinese vases. But it was his servants who entranced me. There were twenty to wait upon a family of three. Agreeable and a garrulous lot, they had a tremendous capacity for idleness. There was Sarkar Babu, whose only function in life seemed to be to work the water pump. This gave him considerable power over the lives of the tenants, a fact which made him behave like a man preoccupied with the weighty cares of the world.

The Cook's Court

To incur his displeasure was tantamount to going without water for the day. The kitchen overlooked a large courtyard at the back of the house and was presided over by a massive-looking cook with a high polished forehead and a disdainful manner. Several adoring young assistants constantly darted around his heels eager to do his bidding. It was they who chopped the vegetables, kneaded the dough, rolled out the rotis, cleaned the fish, ground the masalas and stirred the curries. The cook only ventured forth to officiate over a delicacy, languidly tossing in masalas from a platter held forth by an assistant. Exhausted from the effort, he would retire to his charpoy and sip tea from a large brass tumbler.

The washing was done in the courtyard by a mild-mannered man called Uday, who was helped by a plump lad with a loud guffaw. Uday scoured the vessels and the lad rinsed them. One day the lad disappeared of his own accord and trouble began. Uday, squatting on his haunches, scoured the vessels and then quietly abandoned them. Apparently, under the meek exterior was a rebellious streak. The rinsing was not a part of his job and that was that. The unwashed pile had lain in a sullen, brooding heap for a whole day. The issue became one of honour, with even the assistants refusing to help out. They went around the courtyard, carefully avoiding each other's eyes.

Finally, however, the demands of daily living intervened and the inexhaustible band arrived at their own amiable solution to the problem. Sarkar Babu, unable to suppress his craving for a cup of tea and aware that he could not do so without retrieving a cup, walked across to the garden, picked up the water hose and sprayed the required piece. A ritual was established which prevailed for a whole month until an official assistant was appointed for Uday.

Soon the ritual became a rollicking game with everybody pitching in to take turns with the water jets. The servants did not sit down to dinner before midnight and the real shrieking and singing began only then. For one long shuddering month I remember being woken up to Uday's rendering of "*Bheegi chunariya*". But I survived. Over the years I have forgiven him because he helps summon up remembrances of things past.

All this and much more gave Calcutta its own particular charm. Can I say more?

We had bumped into Chandrakant Shah and his wife in Bombay some years back. They had come down from Cincinnati, Ohio, in order to give their daughter a typical Indian wedding.

THE STORY OF HARRY'S MEND-A-SMILE CLINIC

The Times of India, September 20, 1985

"CALL ME CHUCK," said Chandrakant affably at our first meeting, in a voice that indicated that though his higher education was acquired at an American university, his schooling was pure Paydhuni. Chandrakant had gone to the States in the 50s to study electrical engineering, but finding engineers to be a dime a dozen had switched to selling groceries. The sybaritic splendour of the nuptial arrangements indicated that the choice had been a wise one.

"The bigger the better," he said rubbing his hands. His wife wagged her twin chins in happy agreement. Plump and cheerful, she seemed to accept everything with remarkable placidity. A quarter century spent in America had not infected her with the mulish defiance of women's lib.

"Sure we have real Indian weddings back home," Chandrakant was particular to clarify. "We have your groom on horseback, bride in doli, bhangra dancing baratis and even a Brahmin priest to do the rites. Mind you, not one of those phonies but a real Sanskrit-speaking guy. You just name it and we've got it," he declared

"And who is the lucky young man?" we asked.

"That is the problem," confessed Chandrakant looking at a loss for the first time. But before I could savour his discomfiture, with slightly wicked pleasure, he continued, "The choice boils down to three guys—a doctor, an engineer and a dentist. Actually we like Harish—that's the dentist the best. But... " here the hitch came. With the easy supply of specially treated drinking water threatening to banish tooth decay in America, prospects were bleak for dentists.

"Well!" I said, impressed that in an era of cut-throat competition for eligible grooms and much passing of dowries-under-the-table, Chandrakant could afford to let a detail like reduction in dental cavities stand in the way of his daughter's match.

"But then," said Chandrakant, smiling as though divining my thoughts, "But then, we can pick and choose. We have a green card."

Here he gave a most uncharming chuckle and inhaled deeply at his cigar. It was true. He held the winning hand. Young women with green cards are an irresistible commodity in the marriage market. In return for a few vows by the fire, the girls enable their partners to leap forever into the promised land.

The story has a happy ending. The Shahs finally settled for Harish. We were told that he diversified into cosmetic dentistry and is prospering well on America's obsession for self-improvement. Today Harish is the proud, proprietor of "Harry's Mend a Smile Clinic".

CURZON-SHURZON

The Times of India, September 4, 1985

When I embarked on my thesis in history five years ago no one warned me that my fate hinged on getting it typed. I had no inkling that typists could turn out to be unmanageable in mysterious and esoteric ways. As all thesis writers I had fully developed fantasies about the importance of my research. I was prepared for the mustiness of libraries and for a collection of dark circles around my eyes. And finally, having written out the draft, I had pretty visions of putting my feet up while a typist got on with the job.

This reassuring notion collapsed when the first gentleman returned an otherwise immaculately done draft with my elaborate footnotes mixed up. "Ten, twelve mistakes here and there—what is that?" he said in the pained voice of one more sinned against than sinning.

After some sleepless nights I decided to approach a professional typing agency. History thesis? Yes, indeed, they were fully equipped to handle the matter assured the proprietor thrusting forward a sample of their work. He would come personally the following morning and start the work. But first I would have to pay an advance.

The next day there was no sign of the proprietor and the raw-boned youth he sent instead had but recently passed out of a correspondence course. He set off at great speed, with splendid disregard for punctuation, amputating paragraphs at will and abandoning footnotes that did not fit into the page. He crossed out mistakes with a series of Xs or Ms and when I protested, grudgingly daubed on the whitener leaving a ghoulish smudge behind.

On the third day I called the agency. "I will not tolerate any more of this," I said, "give me back my deposit."

The alacrity with which the proprietor turned up at my door was nothing short of amazing. "Madam," he said, laying his hand on his heart. "Forgive, forgive. I give top class man. Just see."

Mathur was indeed top class. It transpired that he worked in one of the ministries and as a consequence, he assured me, was free all day to take on outside assignments.

"Not like in a private office," he said gleefully. But being top class there were other occupational hazards in dealing with him. He worked on one dozen assignments simultaneously and therefore could only spare me one day in a fortnight.

"Can never say no to anybody," Mathur explained virtuously.

That is how I came to settle for Mr. Mallick: slow, unambitious, retired. But like most elderly men of that generation Mr. Mallick turned out to be a male chauvinist. He believed that women should be sweetly feminine, stay home and not let academia jeopardise domestic bliss. From time to time he would try to wean me away from my pursuit even though it meant endangering his job, losing an income.

The inquisition would begin, "But why do this thesis-phesis? You having house. You having childrens. Husband is affording." Then sternly, "Curzon-Shurzon not get daughter married! Why you want to do thesis-phesis?"

By now I had begun asking myself the same question. For wholly different reasons.

POWDER PUFF

The Times of India, April 22, 1983

I OPENED THE DOOR to a massive hulk of a man clad in dirty white clothes, with hands like shovels. "You the missus?" he asked with a glance of piercing scrutiny. "Mrs. Mehta in Greater Kailash send me to you," he said. I did not dare question the giant for he had already planted one large foot inside my door.

"Okay," he said satisfied with the introduction. "Give one glass water." For a minute I debated whether to risk my house being burgled or my getting punched in the nose. I then opted for the former; insurance companies can be persuaded to cover stolen knick-knacks, but broken bones I felt were a different proposition.

When I returned, he was squatting on his haunches critically peering at a small patch of my verandah mosaic. He had sprayed a flaky white powder over it. Taking the water from my hand, he sprinkled it over the patch. For a whole minute he watched the mixture curdle before swooping down upon it with a large grey handkerchief and rubbing it dry. "Look!" he exulted. "Just you look! Excellent clean, no? All because Magi-Clean!" He thrust a small cardboard packet into my face.

I looked. It was true. In what I had hitherto taken as a clean floor, the singled-out patch stood out in stark, dazzling contrast like things only seem to do in detergent ads in the colour supplements.

By now the booming voice had attracted a sizable crowd in my living room. The servants, my neighbour's mother-in-law and the grocer's delivery boy had collected and were gazing at him in wide-eyed wonder. "Now I go kitchen," he announced.

"Yes, yes," chanted the audience. Once there, with slow deliberation he opened the cabinets, took out the pots and pans and laid them out in a relentless file. "See stains?" he asked, sternly.

"Nowadays which servant clean? How you expect servants clean? Only for nice housewife to clean and clean."

"There has to be acid in your powder," I said provocatively.

But even that could not pierce his merciless armour. With a resigned air he balanced a pinch on his finger and raised it to his mouth. "See clean my teeth. How can have acid?"

"Wah, wah," said the chorus.

"Okay, give me a dozen," I said.

"Only one dozen?" he said in a pained voice. "Your house require minimum four-five dozen. For proper clean. Floor too much dirty."

I tried a different approach.

"Too expensive," I said.

"Oh! ho!" said my inexhaustible salesman. "Money? No take money. For you 1 give free. What is there? Your clean house, my clean house. The audience nodded their heads in affirmation.

I bought six dozen packets.

THE FRAGRANCE REMAINS

The Times of India, August 14, 1985

In a mood for nostalgia I had taken my mother to see her old neighbour and friend Mrs. Singh.

A great desolation had swept over the once ornate flat, the tapestry sofas sagging with sunken springs and the satin curtains looking long unwashed. Mildew crawled along the wall's edge and weeds now trailed from the window boxes. The photographs were everywhere as before, covering the piano and standing three deep on spindly-legged tables. The silver frames had dulled from lack of polish and blotches of dirt smudged the glass.

I picked out a faded portrait of Mr. and Mrs. Singh as newly-weds, their arms intertwined; pictures of their two sons as overfed babies growing to lanky manhood; and several close-ups of the lady herself, younger, stylish, with tight curls and dancing eyes, now at the race course, now languidly masquerading as Cleopatra at a fancy dress ball.

The lustre had dimmed from the eyes she turned to us, sending misgivings into my heart. Was this the same exquisitely turned-out society hostess of my memories hurrying from one fashionable rendezvous to another? She looked so old and forlorn, crouched over a solitary game of cards. As recognition dawned she leapt up, sending her chair crashing to the ground, and rushed forward to grip my mother in a bear hug. The years seemed to melt away; they were once again young housewives living next door to each other, untried by loneliness or tragedy, brimming over with *joie de vivre.*

I thought of the happier days when my brother and I had romped in this home with Mrs. Singh's sons, the boys condescendingly agreeing to include me in their all-male games.

My eyes went to the long wide corridor where priceless China goblets had shivered in their wooden stands as we played a hearty game of indoor cricket. Mrs. Singh's supercilious bearer had reported the matter, subjecting us to confusion, pain and loss of a week's pocket money. His snowy-white eyebrows had now become permanently raised, no doubt stiffened from years of continuous frowning at the world at large. Silent, suspicious, he had stared at me without expression.

I forgave him. He was a part of the nostalgia.

Much water has since passed under the bridge. My younger brother is no more and both Mrs. Singh's sons have settled abroad. But the ladies chatted as though their tale could have no ending, with no recrimination against the merciless sequence of their destiny.

It was time to say goodbye. "Wait," ordered Mrs. Singh, her voice by now having regained most of its strength and penetrative vigour. She disappeared into her bedroom and returned with an old bottle of scent, and pressed it into my mother's hand.

"Don't think I've forgotten," she declared. "I remember it is your birthday. This is all I have to give you today."

Some of the perfume may have evaporated but the fragrance remains.

IMPERIAL POMP & CIRCUMSTANCE

The Hindustan Times, October 11, 1981

Gone are the days of the Raj when the band played haunting Viennese waltzes to richly attired guests. Now the receptions are a sedate, democratic affair with guests quietly munching limp samosas and queuing up for hot cups of tea.

The imposing Viceregal "thrones": the pomp and panoply of office made young Mary Curzon gushingly write to her parents "... for all fuss and ceremony we might as well be monarchs."

The arched gateway of Government House, Calcutta, with a lion atop. It is now the Raj Bhavan, Kolkata.

A view of the Government House from south.

The interior of Government House with marble busts of long-ago Roman Caesers.

THOSE WERE GLITTERING evenings—when horse-drawn carriages drove guests through the massive wrought-iron gates, up the gravel drive for a State Dinner at Calcutta's viceregal residence, the Government House. Outside, the temperature may have been a 100 degrees Fahrenheit but the perspiring guests dared not slacken in their formal attire; a glance of viceregal displeasure was tantamount to cancellation of future invitations. There would be uniformed generals, their chests sagging with medals from the Afghan Wars; an occasional maharaja in jewels and brocade; men in tight silk breeches; and ladies in billowing satin dresses, loaded with jewellery.

Walking on crimson carpets the guests went to the vast Marble Hall and toward the throne-like chairs where their viceregal hosts awaited them—he in a jewelled sky-blue cloak and the sashes of office, she in a flowing gown with a blazing tiara on her head. Baskets of orchids, and palm trees in large brass pots framed the windows. At intervals, standing rigidly to attention, were the Viceroy's Bodyguards—handsome, six-foot, fierce-looking men in scarlet tunics, jack boots and blue and gold pugris. A female English visitor sighed as she recorded in her dairy. "For looks I don't believe they have their equal in the world." Dinner for guests numbering upto 120 could be a sit-down affair with gold-plate on the sideboard and a footman behind every chair.

The kitchen was a five-minute walk from the dining hall. The food was in covered wooden boxes slung from poles and carried by two servants each. If they were not careful, it was likely to be gobbled up by the foxes and the jackals which habitually prowled the grounds every night.

Completed in 1803 by Lord Wellesley, Calcutta's Government House was certainly an imposing residence worthy of the highest representative of British authority in India. Like most imperial architecture, Government House sought to keep up "an outward appearance of power" to "save the necessity of resort to the actual exercise of it." Wellesley was severely criticised by the directors of the East India Company for what they thought was a wasteful and unnecessary expense. It had cost Rs.12 lakhs in those days. Wellesley is said to have haughtily answered: "I wish India to be ruled from a palace, not from a counting house; with the ideas of a Prince, not with those of a retail dealer in indigo." The directors of the East India Company, however, did have cause for indignation. The construction of the Government House had started on February 5. 1799 and it was not until 1802 that they came to know of Wellesley's plan.

By sheer coincidence the design, prepared by a Captain Wyatt of the Bengal Engineers, was based on Lord Curzon's ancestral home, Kedleston Hall in Derbyshire. On a visit to Calcutta as a young Conservative M.P. of 28 in 1887, Curzon was struck by its marked resemblance to his ancestral seat, and loftily declared that he would next return as Viceroy. In fact it took him three more visits to India to achieve that ambition. Nevertheless, he was only 39 when he was installed as the youngest Viceroy in Government House.

It is magnificent even today. There is cold perfection in the white and gold Marble Hall with tinkling chandeliers and its marching file of 20 fluted columns. The hall opens onto a smaller saloon, called the Throne Room, which soars upwards to a silver dome. It was here that the Viceroy received his official visitors, from his silver throne, with lion-heads for armrests,

When the Muslim League was founded with the blessings of Lord Minto, Lady Minto noted in her diary that her husband's action had prevented "sixty two millions of people from joining the ranks of the Seditious Opposition".

The indolent Lord Lytton scandalised Calcutta society by sneaking off into the Throne Room for a quick smoke in the middle of a state function.

shielded by a canopy of scarlet velvet. Only for a 21-gun salute for a maharaja did he descend the steps of his throne and walk to the edge of the gold carpet to receive his royal guest.

There was no electricity until 1899 and gas-light was used. Lady Canning found that the best way of keeping the heat out was by shutting "every chink of window" at half-past seven in the morning, by putting down the venetian blind, and hanging up the khus tatties outside every door. Breeze was provided by the cloth punkhas suspended from the ceiling and operated by punkha-wallahs who sat outside, silent and uncomplaining, pulling the cords monotonously with their big toes.

Until 1905 there was only one bathroom with running water, with a hierarchy of servants: one heated the water, another fetched the tub, a third filled it, and a fourth emptied it.

The maintenance of this vast establishment involved no less than 700 servants, according to a rough estimate. Yvonne Fitzroy, Secretary to Lady Reading, writes that this vast staff was "ruled by the Viceroy's Private Secretary..."

By the time Lord Reading came to India as Viceroy, the imperial capital had shifted to Delhi. Nevertheless, the rules governing the viceregal household remained largely unchanged. There was also the Comptroller, and in Miss Fitzroy's words, "to him it fell to scan the accounts, to check the spoons, to sack the servants, to preside over the yearly migration to the hills, and then to preside over it back again to keep everyone in a good temper, to give us chairs to sit on, beds to sleep in, home truths from time to time, and food to eat."

So perfect was their management, however, that Lady Reading was prompted to record in admiration how upon arriving at a new destination she found that "Your own servants are there behind your chair for a four-course breakfast and even your favourite chair and cushion on the verandah to meet you." Only the Russian Tsars were known to have enjoyed such luxuries.

The Viceroy was called upon to do much entertaining in his official capacity. Curzon with his fussy meticulousness totted up the number of meals served at the Government House to visitors and inmates in the month of January 1899 alone to 3,500. Twenty-two years later, in the month of December, as many as 1,115 bottles of champagne were consumed here, even though by now it enjoyed the diminished status of being merely the home of a Governor General. Curzon wrote to a colleague in England within the first month of his sojourn in India in January 1899, "It is three weeks since I assumed office tomorrow. Within that time we have had a levee Drawing-Room, State Ball, State Evening Party, three big dinners for sixty, and four or more of 20-30, so we have not been idle."

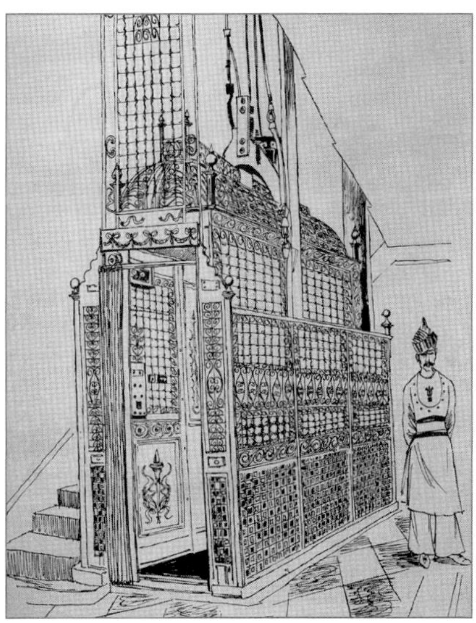

Bird cage at Government House (Illustration by Desmond Doig).

The various vicereines almost seemed to have taken a martyr's delight in their lot. Lady Canning wrote, "These dinners are very wearisome. Neither C. nor I can get at all the people. Not a man has ever voluntarily spoken to me since I came to India... and the ladies look terribly afraid of me."

In long-suffering tones, they complained of the heat and the loneliness but almost all thrived on the adulation they received; the power, pomp and pageantry more than compensated for the discomfort of a tropical land. Emily Eden, sister of Governor General Auckland, grumbled about the inescapable presence of silent native servants in constant attendance. The Curzon children, however, wholeheartedly enjoyed this attention. Years later, Irene Curzon was to write happily of how, when they drove in a landau on the grounds of the Government House, they were accompanied by three nurses, two liveried men on the box and two standing up behind. Sometimes their army of attendants included a good-natured Viceroy's policeman "who usually carried one or two of our broken-legged dolls!"

The famed massive staircase at the Government House, guarded by two sphinxes and leading up to the portico with eight Corinthian columns was used only for the arrival and departure of a viceroy. Then it used to be swathed in crimson, carpeted and lined on both sides, according to rank by the highest ranking civilians, army officers, princes and other dignitaries of state. Right at the bottom waited the Governor of Bengal, and at the top, the outgoing Viceroy. The cannons of Fort William boomed the 31-gun salute as the new Viceroy made his slow, measured ascent up the steps to the heady pinnacle of power. It must have indeed seemed like a journey to heaven.

The Government House lost some of its splendour in 1912 with the moving of the capital to Delhi. The Throne Room where the indolent, bizarre Lord Lytton had, by closeting himself there to puff at a cigarette in the middle of a state levee, scandalised Calcutta Society, now remains a museum-piece. The great dome above has been sealed off, some say to make storage space. The quaint lift with its exquisite filigree metal-work, popularly known as "the bird's cage" continues to heave its majestic way up and down. The vast hierarchy of servants has been considerably reduced. Old retainers, however, still wear gorgeously braided uniforms and dream of the days gone by. Marble-topped tables and heavy ebony sofas abound, reminders of another age. But on the walls hang portraits of the leader of independent India.

Official parties no longer go on till the early hours of the morning with the band playing haunting Viennese waltzes and guests in various stages of drunken stupor having to be discreetly put into their carriages by footmen. Now the receptions are sedate, democratic, one-hour affairs with guests quietly munching limp samosas and sandesh and queuing up for cups of hot tea.

Curzon's ancestral home, Kedleston Hall, UK, which was used as the model for building the Government House in Calcutta. Upon seeing this, Curzon, said, "Next time I shall not come as a guest but as the Viceroy of India. He did just that at age 39!

PARTITION OF BENGAL & THE GENESIS OF PAKISTAN

The Hindustan Times, October 22, 2005

THE LEGENDARY BELIEF IN the 'fairness' of the British was shattered on October 16, 1905—the day of Lord Curzon's Partition of Bengal—and is regarded as a turning point in British India's history. Curzon made it out to be an administrative decision to relieve an overburdened state. But Indian opinion has always viewed the Viceroy's act as a Machiavellian measure to 'divide and rule' India by tearing apart the province along communal lines, giving birth to a Muslim-majority province in the east.

The rise of Calcutta as the capital of the Empire had enhanced the status of the Hindu bhadralok. But now the British began to have second thoughts. Partitioning Bengal was neither a new idea nor Curzon's brainchild. Upon assuming his viceroyalty, Curzon had said, "Bengal is unquestionably too large a charge for any single man," as it included Bihar and Orissa and a population of 78 million. He favoured the option of enlarging the Central Provinces by giving up territory from Bengal, Berar, Orissa and Ganjam districts of Madras. But the secretaries in the Viceroy's council convinced him of the political advantage of dividing the province on communal lines, which would result in removing "a solid body of opponents" to our rule.

Within two years, the transfer turned into a full-scale partition, with not merely the Chittagong division, but also Dacca, Mymensingh, Rajshahi division, Malda and Tippera Hills going into the new province of East Bengal and Assam, while Bihar and Orissa remained with Bengal.

There was widespread protest throughout the country that the partition was politically motivated. Keen to woo Muslim support in the eastern province, the Viceroy had enthusiastically turned his attention to the largest Muslim landowner, Nawab Salimullah of Dacca, and told him how the new province, with Dacca as its capital, "would invest the Mohammedans of Eastern Bengal with a unity which they had not enjoyed since the days of the old Musalman viceroys and kings." What is perhaps more shocking and not so well known is that the Viceroy gave a loan or £100,000 to set the seal for endorsement.

On July 19 that year, the final scheme for partition was declared. "The announcement fell like a bombshell upon

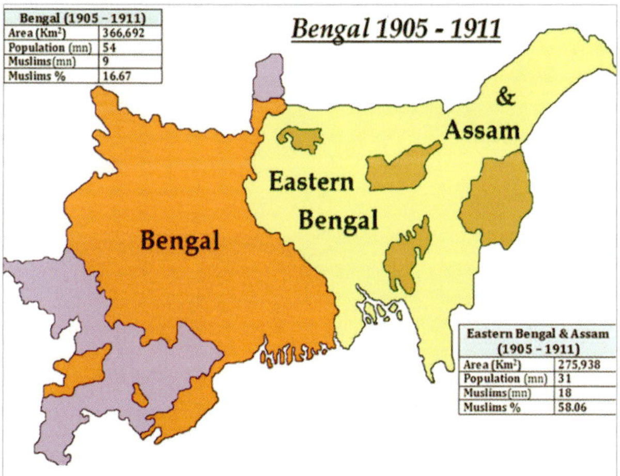

Map showing the new boundaries of Bengal after the Partition of 1905.

an astonished public," cried moderate nationalist leader, Surendranath Banerjea. "We felt we had been insulted, humiliated and tricked." Overnight, a new spirit of patriotism filled the air. Bonfires were made of British goods, swadeshi schools sprang up and indigenous companies began to manufacture swadeshi goods. So charged was the air that it became dangerous to appear in foreign clothing.

By day, brave young men came out on the streets to picket bazaars and enforce the boycott. At night, the streets were eerie and deserted; sometimes the flames of burning Manchester cloth could be seen glowing in the darkness. The Viceroy shut his eyes to the new mood of confidence sweeping across Asia: a mood which was focused by the Japanese triumph over Russia that had shattered the myth of European invincibility.

An aggressive new militancy was taking over the reins of nationalism.

Even before sunrise on October 16, the day of the partition, Calcutta's streets had begun echoing with the cries of '*Bande Mataram*'. Patriotic sentiments shot up to an all-time high. Virtual strangers stopped each other on the streets to tie rakhis, symbolising brotherhood. But in the new province of Eastern Bengal and Assam, the new Lieutenant Governor, Sir Bampfylde Fuller, was busy igniting the fire of separatism. When Fuller declared, "I was like a man who was married to two wives, one a Hindu, the other a Muhammadan—both young and charming—but was forced into the arms of one of them by the rudeness of the other," angry agitators threatened to tie a garland of old shoes around his neck. When the Government of India, in due course,

The flames of burning Manchester cloth could be seen in many places.

Local newspapers mourned that their 'motherland' had been cut up into pieces.

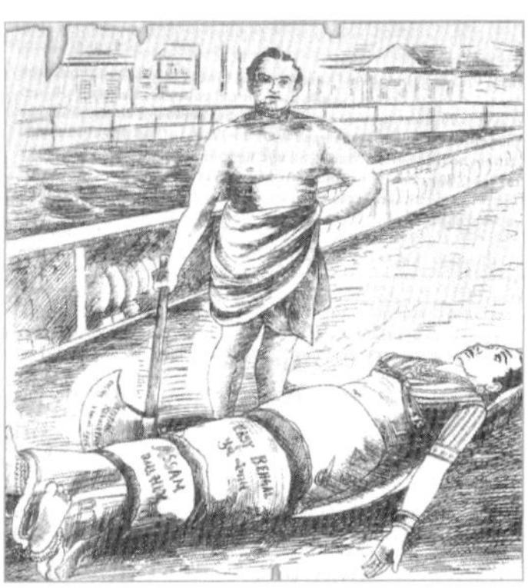

Congregation of 30,000 Muslim supporters of the new province.

Bande Mataram

Weekly Edition.

PUBLISHED EVERY SUNDAY.

VOL. I. CALCUTTA, SUNDAY, SEPTEMBER 29, 1907. NO. 16.

OUR PICTURE GALLERY.

SJT. AUROBINDO GHOSE.

Aurobindo took control of inflammatory newspaper "Bande Mataram". He preached in so lofty a style that thousands flocked to his side.

pressurised Fuller to resign, a massive meeting of 30,000 Muslims at Dacca passed a resolution deploring his resignation.

By February 1906, the lean and fanatical Aurobindo Ghose had returned to Calcutta to set into motion revolutionary terrorism on Irish lines. He became the leader of the extremist group in the Congress party and was soon demanding the absolute right of self-determination for the people of India. Overnight, the towns and the countryside in Bengal were honeycombed with terrorist societies, the Dacca Anushilan alone boasting 500 branches. The severity of the agitation further aggravated the growing divide, drawing the Nawab of Dacca into closer cooperation with the Aligarh group of Sir Sayyid Ahmed Khan, who has sought a separate platform for Muslims as early as in 1869. Historian professor Ikram, in his book *Modern Muslim India and the Birth of Pakistan* (Delhi, 1950), was prophetic when he said, "The Nawab's invitation brought the Aligarh leadership to the heart of Muslim Bengal, which marked the turning point in the history of the subcontinent. This was the genesis of Pakistan."

A few months later in December 1906, the All India Muslim League was founded in Dacca with Nawab Salimullah playing the lead role. Muslim opinion began to move sharply away from the national mainstream, having found itself a new platform in the League. Nationalism began to strike a hammer blow at the roots of British power, and separatism threatened Indian unity, culminating in the creation of Pakistan, neither of which were consequences Curzon intended.

The partition of Bengal was revoked in 1911. But the damage had been done. The six year partition laid the foundation of a permanant division and rang the death knell of the Raj. The Muslim majority province of Eastern Bengal—barring Assam, Goalpara and Cachar—ended up becoming a Muslim majority nation, first as East Pakistan in 1947, and then Bangladesh in 1971. It is hardly surprising that Calcutta is not yet ready to forgive the Viceroy for his Partition of 1905.

The writer is author of Lord Curzon: Last of the British Moghuls, *(OUP).*

THE DELHI DURBAR, 1911

A grandiloquent gesture to proclaim the power and panoply of the Raj at High Noon. It also marked two momentous announcements.

Commemorative obelisk erected at the exact same spot as the royal pavilion.

The elaborate royal pavilion where King George and Queen Mary sat enthroned, receiving homage from the Indian royals.

King George V makes a state entry but because people were expecting him atop an elephant, scant notice was taken of the monarch to his dismay.

So began the building of New Delhi, a metropolis of grandeur and beauty.

LAST HURRAH OF THE RAJ

Exactly one hundred years ago, Delhi was witness to a dazzling spectacle—an Imperial Durbar, the magnificence of which the world had rarely seen. Held in what is now known as Coronation Park in North Delhi, it celebrated the visit to India and the coronation of the King Emperor George V and his consort. The Durbar was a grandiloquent gesture to proclaim the power and panoply of a Raj at High Noon.

There was a popular saying at the turn of the 19th century: 'The Sun never sets on the British Empire'. World War I, which saw the collapse of mighty European empires, was still three years away. Britannia ruled the waves and India was its most precious prize. As 1911 dawned, the only dark cloud over the government of India were those left in the wake of Lord Curzon's Machiavellian Partition of Bengal in 1905. Ostensibly taken for administrative convenience, Indian national opinion saw it as part of the 'divide and rule' policy.

The founding of the Muslim League with the blessings of Curzon's successor Lord Minto in 1906 only served to endorse the fear. The resulting militant nationalist agitation spread far and wide. Vernacular newspapers inflamed youthful passions and secret societies mushroomed across the countryside. "A cruel wrong has been inflicted upon our Bengali brethren and the whole country has been stirred to its deepest depth with sorrow and resentment as has never been the case before," protested the usually moderate Gopal Krishna Gokhale, President of the Indian National Congress.

The new Viceroy, Lord Minto, like his predecessor, upheld the partition, convinced that its revocation would be taken as surrendering to agitation and lowering the prestige of the Raj. Governmental policy hovered, therefore, between repressive legislation, deportation without trial, and conciliatory gestures, hoping for the 'mists to lift' and 'the roseate days' of British rule to return. When, however, the first ingenuously produced bomb was exploded in Muzaffarpur in 1908, the government recognised it as a wake-up call for John Bull. A nervous Secretary of State for India, Lord Morley, warned the Viceroy that "The villainy of the bombs makes a new situation for us... the old days are gone... we cannot carry on upon the old maxims." The wife and daughter of an English pleader were killed in the attack. Of the two assassins, one committed suicide and the other, 18-year-old Khudiram Bose, was sent to the gallows, but not before he had become a national martyr. Students went into mourning and his photograph was sold in the markets.

The chain of political assassinations continued unabated. The Mintos had a narrow escape when their carriage was bombed in Ahmedabad. So did the Hardinges as they made a State Entry into Delhi in 1912. His attendant was killed instantaneously.

Lord Hardinge succeeded Minto as Viceroy in November 1910. An astute career diplomat, Hardinge realised the need to calm the agitators, although he was initially reluctant to reverse Curzon's decision as it would be tantamount to giving in "to the noisy clamour" of the revolutionaries. But six months later the Viceroy said, "Nothing could be worse... than the condition of Assam and Eastern Bengal." The new Viceroy had got down to work preparing for the

Durbar, confessing, however, that it would be "an immense relief" when the royal visit was over.

Then New Delhi was a barren wasteland. As a visitor to the 1911 Durbar said, "Delhi lay on a malarial plain surrounded by melancholy vestiges of ruined and departed alien greatness." Soon, Delhi turned into a fortress as thousands of tents came up to shelter the 562 Indian princes with their priceless jewels and fabled entourages.

On December 2, 1911, the royal party sailed into Bombay. There was a minor hiccup at the time of the King's State Entry into Delhi. The King had chosen to ride a horse and his presence went unnoticed by those who expected a royal elephant in full regalia. Seeing the Viceroy atop an elephant, the crowds exclaimed, "There is the Lord Sahib. But where is the King?" Hardinge was to note that although the King tried making salaams, "he was disappointed at his non-recognition by the people." All the Indian rulers were present—exotic, flamboyant, some enlightened, some decadent, glorying in the tales of wealth and peccadilloes. Apart from their palaces in India, they frequently maintained houses in London, Paris and the Riviera.

Some were enlightened rulers who worked ceaselessly for the emancipation of the people. The Gaekwad of Baroda, like the Nizam of Hyderabad, enjoyed the privilege of a 21-gun salute. He established colleges and schools and encouraged the emancipation of women and untouchables. Despite his impressive cavalcade, the Gaekwad was noted not to have made adequate obeisance to the King. Incidentally, the Gaekwad was known to have provided a safe haven to many militant nationalists, including Sri Aurobindo, who was the high priest of the agitation in Bengal.

Nawab Osman Ali Khan, Nizam of Hyderabad, was conspicuous by his presence. Considered among the world's richest men, he is said to have restricted his personal expenditure to cigarettes and betel nut. He wore the same fez cap for thirty-five years. After his death, his son found the Jacob's diamond in the toe of an old slipper.

Surprisingly it was the king himself who played the leading role in revoking the partition. When the time came for the monarch to declare the royal boon to his people, he had risen to his feet at the sound of trumpets and the roll of drums. In a loud and clear voice he made the historic announcement that Bengal will be unified and the Imperial capital would be transferred from Calcutta to Delhi. The announcement fell like a bombshell upon the unsuspecting public. On the one hand it seemed that Bengal had won its battle, but by depriving it of its prestige as the capital, it was a hollow victory. Nevertheless, the escape to Delhi bespoke a sign of retreat by the Raj. True enough 36 years later, the sun set on the Empire and India ceased to be the brightest jewel in the British Crown.

Hardinge, who had initially scoffed at the King's suggestion, saying it was "quite impracticable", had quickly discovered that "anarchy is far from dead" in India. The revolutionaries driven underground were on the warpath.

Eventually it was this seemingly hopeless situation on the ground that persuaded Hardinge to change his mind and confess to the Secretary of State, "The results anticipated... have not been attained... the political power of the Bengalis has not been broken ... they will never cease to agitate until they have obtained a modification of the partition."

Curzon was kept in the dark till the end. Later he was to thunder in Parliament, ranting at his

Today, the statues of the monarchs, viceroys and other Raj grandees stand, stately but forlorn, in the Coronation Park in North Delhi.

successors for hiding behind the person of the King. He said, "You invest it with a sacrosanct character by putting it in the mouth of the sovereign... you have done it in a manner that saves you from retribution and screens you from attack." These historic announcements added significance to the Durbar of 1911, for they are said to have had a profound effect on the future of modern Indian history.

Thirty-six years later Pandit Nehru was sworn in as Prime Minister of Independent India and the British government left our shores forever. The old superstition proved to be inexorably true—that no ruling party that shifted its seat of government to the ancient capital that was Delhi survived for long.

Thus began the building of New Delhi, a metropolis of immense grandeur and beauty.

King George's statue has lost its commanding position on Kingsway/Rajpath where he had been the monarch of all he surveyed. It now lingers at Coronation Park in stately but forlorn majesty along with statues of other viceroys. They probably hold little meaning for India's young generation; however, they are part and parcel of 300 years of Indian history and it would be churlish on our part as modern, vibrant and emancipated Indians to deny them a fitting requiem.

It is fitting that Coronation Park is being readied to receive these Empire builders of yore. There they will be preserved for young India to witness the unfolding of their colonial past.

MOMENTS TO REMEMBER

Myself, aged eleven.

With my mother, Savitri Daftary, just before leaving for America.

Manjula and Dwarkadas, my parents-in-law, who lovingly looked after my daughters as I went in search of Curzon.

"Meet the son-in-law"

Excitement over the first grandchild

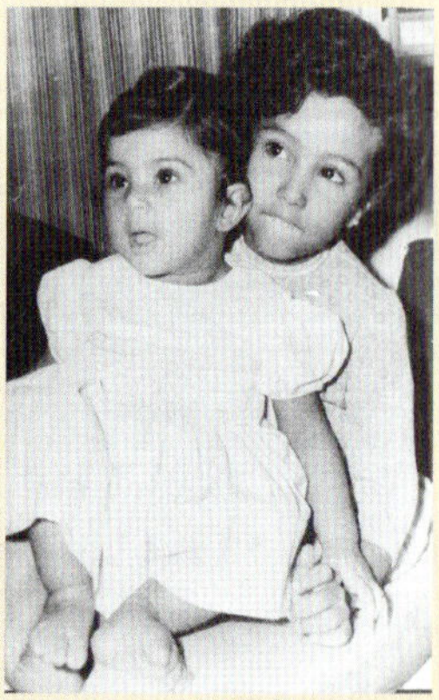

Madhavi and Brinda.

Two sisters.

On a trip to Agra

Halycon Cambridge days: Brinda & Madhavi at their graduations.

Brinda's wedding to Gautam Shroff: To pull the jamai babu's nose, a one time prerogative of the mother-in law!

Madhavi marries Shyam Divan.

Gautam and Brinda swinging away!

Selena, Prafull, Avanti, Nayana, Ahan, Brinda, Devaki, Madhavi, Shyam and Gautam.

Ahan, Devaki and Selena: Anchors ahoy!

Madhavi with her two cherubs.

Ahan Shroff and Devaki Divan's tug of war over rakhi. In our home, a brother also ties a rakhi to his sister!

Prafull and Nayana: Made for each other!

Avanti Divan, a Princeton graduate.

Selena Shroff, our freshly minted graduate.

And the story goes on...of life, love and laughter!

ACKNOWLEDGEMENTS

Prafull, my anchor for everything, always.
Brinda and Madhavi for their overweening, at times exasperating, but always loving concern which makes them all the more precious.
Gautam and Shyam for their affection, understanding and support, always.
Avanti, Selena, Devaki and Ahan, my adorables — what would I do without you?

The editors of *The Times of India, The Statesman, The Hindustan Times, The Illustrated Weekly of India, Imprint* for their graciously letting me use my articles here. Also Prafull Goradia for allowing me to use extracts from his autobiography *Fly me to the Moon* (Bloomsbury India, 2017).

The late Mario Miranda for illustrating two articles of mine.
Namita Gokhale, my motivator and always a dear friend.
Sarayu and Sarla, my "didis" for their encouragement.
Aditya for writing the preface.
Devaki Divan for her editorial input.
Malini Saigal for the elegant design which brings that extra dimension to the book.
Ranjan Puhan for typing out the manuscript.